Voyages With a Merchant Prince

To Gill Wood

Best Wishes

From Ivy Hutchinson

May 2012

Voyages with a Merchant Prince

Secrets of the Ripley Diary

J.M. & M.F. Hutchinson

ISBN 978-1475238426

Printed in the United States of America.

Contents

List of Illustrations

1

Planning the Voyage of a Lifetime

In the summer of 1830 Thomas Ripley, a Liverpool shipowner, set sail on a voyage that would make his fortune. Thomas, who grew up in a sailors' tavern, had big dreams of making a great deal of money, and he had the energy and the audacity to make them come true. This is his story.

The ship he sailed in was a fine three-masted vessel, owned by Ripley himself. Thomas decided he would take his young wife with him. Together they set out on a journey that would change many lives. When they boarded the ship and said farewell to Liverpool, the young couple were excited by the idea of all the experiences that lay ahead of them, the exotic foreign countries they would visit, the sights they would see, the wildlife and the scenery, the new foods they might taste, and the people they would meet.

Thomas knew that they would encounter all sorts of dangers on the way. Julia was aware that the sea voyage to China was hazardous and the threat from pirates was real, but she was prepared to face rough seas and deprivation to be with Tom and to experience adventure. She did not know that her husband had hired a rebellious crew, and the hardships of the voyage would drive them to mutiny.

The Princes Dock, Liverpool.
Lancashire Illustrated (1831)

Thomas Ripley was born in 1790, in the town of Lancaster, which was a thriving port in the eighteenth century.[1] For a child with a love of shipping, Lancaster was an exciting place to be. There were shipyards too in Lancaster, where the rasp of saws and the ring of the shipwrights' hammers resounded across Green Ayre. Vessels up to about 300 tons were built there.

At this time Lancaster traded mainly with the West Indies. There was a lot of money made in the slave trade. Vessels left the port on the notorious triangular route: they picked up slaves on the coast of Africa, sailed on to the West Indies to sell their unfortunate human cargo, then returned to Lancaster with cotton, rum, sugar, and mahogany. It was on this trade that the town's prosperity was based. When the slave trade was banned in 1807, direct trade with the West Indies continued. Ships brought back tortoiseshell and elephants 'teeth' (ivory tusks), cochineal and indigo from the Bahamas and oranges and lemons from the Azores.[2]

In this thriving, bustling market town there was plenty of prosperity for many people, but on a small scale. Wealthy merchants favoured the new Georgian houses in Church Street, but poorer areas like China Lane, where the Ripley family lived, also benefited from the custom generated by the overseas trade.

Thomas Ripley's father James was a vigorous fellow, a victualler, who ran and owned a pub called the Three Tuns. This successful innkeeper also owned other small properties in and around Lancaster. In 1798 James had been married for over eleven years to Nancy Irwin.[3] They had eight healthy children, six sons and two daughters.[4] Thomas was their fourth child, then aged seven. On March the 29th, Thomas's father suddenly found himself close to death. Hastily he sent for his solicitor to make a will, he signed with a shaking hand and died later that day.[5] He was just forty-four years old.[6] He had left enough to provide modest security for his widow and children. Tom's mother Nancy took over the management of the pub. She must have been made of stern stuff, to take on the running of a dockside tavern with its rough clientele. She had to supervise employees, and manage tenants who lived at the back of the pub, as well as bringing up her eight children, the youngest of whom was only two years old. In the 1790s there were no laws to prevent children from mixing with the customers in the pub. Thomas and his siblings would have heard all the gossip about the latest vessel to arrive at the docks, which were only a few minutes walk away. Seamen from the ships came and drank in the Three Tuns and astonished the locals with their stories of storms and shipwrecks and faraway foreign places.

By the terms of her husband's will Nancy was allowed to remain living in The Three Tuns, in China Lane until her youngest child, Henry, attained twenty-one years, if she remained James Ripley's "chaste widow". Nancy had other ideas. Three years later she married Edmund Pugh, a local plasterer, on 20 August 1801.[7] Cunning manoeuvring on Nancy's part ensured that she stayed in China Lane, managing the pub, even after her second marriage, and in fact she was later recorded as the pub's owner.[8]

James Ripley had made provisions to pay for his children's schooling.[9] At the end of the eighteenth century many people were still illiterate. Parents who could afford even rudimentary schooling for their children felt that literacy and numeracy were first steps to better paid employment and to making a good marriage. Thomas got his first lucky break when he left school and was apprenticed to a merchant called Thomas Burrow, who became the Mayor of Lancaster in 1805.[10] Thomas Ripley was fourteen that year, the age at which an apprenticeship typically began. Burrow was the most influential merchant in Lancaster at that time. He was intent on industrialising Lancaster and he had the wealth to do this. In 1802 he had provided the financial backing for building the town's first steam-powered mill.[11] The Burrow family were also shipowners and had money in a cotton factory, grocery and linen-drapery shops.[12] Burrow made his money in the West Indies trade and had business contacts in Demerara.[13] This apprenticeship was to give Thomas Ripley an insight into the world of shipping that would help him to make his own fortune later on.

Trade with the West Indies was fraught with danger during

4

the Napoleonic Wars, but it was so lucrative that merchants insisted on sending their ships despite the increased risks. For protection ships sailed in convoys with a naval escort. On her maiden voyage to Tortola, in 1806, Burrow and Mason's new ship the *Abram* was 'expected to proceed with the first convoy from Cork after February the 1st.'[14] On 20 February the convoy of one hundred and forty vessels sailed from Cork under the protection of *HMS Mediator* and the sloop *Squirrel*, bound for the West Indies. The French were always on the lookout for a vulnerable vessel. A Lancaster ship the *Robert*, was involved in a two and a half hour chase at sea before she was ultimately captured.[15]

As Burrow's apprentice, Thomas Ripley learned about the risks and rewards of the West Indies trade. Those ships that made it home safely brought luxury goods that commanded high prices. The successful merchant was gratified by the sight of his barrels of sugar and hogsheads and puncheons of choice Jamaica and Antigua rum being unloaded on the quayside.[16] Subsequent sales of goods and even of vessels were often negotiated at the merchants' coffee room in Lancaster.[17]

The people of Lancaster followed the events of the war with Napoleon closely. Lord Nelson was the nation's hero and communities in trading ports had a special and vested interest in naval victory. After the battle of Trafalgar in 1805, the news of Nelson's death was a bitter blow. On the day of Nelson's funeral the flag was hoisted to half-mast above Saint Mary's Church, Lancaster, and 'the great bell tolled every minute during the day'.[18]

In the same year Thomas Ripley lost his stepfather. Edmund Pugh had been married to Nancy for just four years before his death. Nevertheless, he had become very attached to his stepchildren in that time, especially as he had no other children of his own. He provided generously for the Ripley children in his

5

will. William Ripley, who was not the eldest, happened to be Edmund's favourite; to William he left two hundred pounds. To the other children, James, George, Thomas, John, Nancy, Jenny and Henry, he left a hundred pounds each. This sum was to be paid to each child when they became twenty-one. The residue of Edmund Pugh's estate was over a thousand pounds and this all went to his widow Nancy.[19]

The Ripley children were also due to inherit a hundred pounds each from their own father when they came of age. The two girls would have used this money to help secure a good marriage. As married women, Nancy and Jenny preferred to be known as Ann and Jane; more formal names that reflected their new status in society.

The brothers had several options: they could use the money to buy some modest property to give them security, they could invest the money and live on the income, or they could risk the whole sum in some business venture of their own. George chose the comparative safety of the legal profession. Thomas, William and John decided to risk all and go into business together.

The first evidence of the brothers' commercial activities is in 1811-12. The records show that William and Thomas were in business with another merchant called Jackson, and that they "occupied a house in Sun Street as counting house and warehouse for trade".[20] When John came of age in 1813, he joined his brothers as a partner in their trading activities, and went out to the West Indies to live. Like other tropical colonies, the island of St. Thomas, where John settled, was a dangerous place for Europeans, who often succumbed to disease. Like many men, he was prepared to take that risk because the rewards were so high, and the brothers needed someone they could trust to take care of business at that end. Some time before 1817 Jackson was bought out, or chose to leave the partnership, and the business became known as "Ripley Brothers and Co.".[21]

During the Napoleonic Wars the demand for uniforms kept trade in Lancashire buoyant, but even so there were some people whose businesses did not survive. The failure of a small business could be catastrophic for the owners in the days before limited liability legislation. In addition to losing his business premises, the bankrupt would lose his house if he owned one, and he would have the humiliation of seeing his personal possessions advertised for auction in the local newspaper. Everything from mahogany furniture to eight-day clocks, feather beds and bedsteads, were auctioned off on behalf of the creditors.[22]

With the end of the Napoleonic Wars, a recession set in. 'With the cessation of war in 1815 came glutted markets, for demand stopped while production went on. Shipping suffered. For commerce the result was naturally disastrous and a great wave of ruin swept over the country'.[23] Bad weather brought poor harvests, and the economic situation grew worse. Throughout 1816 the number of bankruptcies in Lancaster increased and towards the end of that year several were reported in the newspaper every week. The Ripley brothers hung on throughout the worst months, hoping to survive until trade improved. Right at the very end of 1817 the business succumbed and the brothers were declared bankrupt.

The ignominious bankruptcy notice appeared in the local paper. It read:

"To be sold by auction at the King's Arms Inn in Lancaster …authorised in and by a commission of bankrupt … on Monday the 15th of December at six o'clock in the evening … a freehold warehouse situated on the east side of Sun Street in Lancaster, with stable, yard, and premises thereto belonging late in the possession of Messrs Ripley Brothers and Co."[24]

In striking contrast to other bankruptcies, no personal possessions or properties were listed, and the warehouse was *empty of merchandise*. The brothers may have skilfully contrived to minimise their losses. Had they pre-empted the declaration of bankruptcy by selling off what they could themselves? It was most fortuitous for them that their mother Nancy Pugh now owned the pub, even though this was not what their father had originally intended.[25] It meant that the pub did not have to be included in the assets to be sold off to meet the brothers' debts. The Three Tuns did not go under the hammer.

Even though the brothers' losses could have been worse, the bankruptcy was still a bitter and humiliating defeat. Thomas never forgot the day of the auction at the King's Arms. The loss of the business in 1817 only served to fuel his ambition for wealth and success, which he intended to achieve by any means, no matter how reckless. The small town of Lancaster no longer seemed to offer Thomas the opportunities he was looking for.

2

The Leaving of Liverpool

Liverpool was a magnet to young men in the nineteenth century. It was a port of growing national importance. The stagecoach left Lancaster for Liverpool every day from outside the Bear Inn.[26] Thomas resolved to go to Liverpool and make a fresh start there. He left Lancaster as 'a poor young man' of twenty-seven but he held on to the hope that he would, in time, make his fortune.[27]

Liverpool was shaking off the eighteenth century. Its dark narrow streets were being widened and paved and new docks were being built. New public buildings had recently appeared; a larger town hall, libraries and a corn exchange. From a vantage point near the village of Everton "the town of Liverpool was displayed in nearly its full extent, on the right a range of elegant houses with shrubberies and gardens, and in front an extensive view of the Mersey ... and a partial view of the northern coast of Lancashire, on a clear day Wales could be discerned".[28] A newcomer to Liverpool would no doubt have been impressed by the docks, which could hold up to nine hundred vessels at one time.[29] The docks presented "a striking picture of the extent of human power when directed by mechanical contrivance".[30] These modern marvels were soon to make Liverpool one of the world's foremost maritime ports.

Thomas arrived in Liverpool in 1818. George Ripley, Tom's brother, was already there and was practising as an attorney in Seymour Street. Thomas took some premises in Bold Street in the centre of town, where many businesses were located.[31] At the lower end of Bold Street there was a large subscription library, known as the Lyceum, which housed twenty-two thousand volumes. More importantly for a merchant, it also boasted a spacious coffee house.[32] Pubs in the business district were beginning to open up dining rooms where busy merchants could buy their midday meal. The Palace Inn in nearby Lord Street was later to claim that it had been the first to offer this service 'to those gentlemen whose business prevents them from dining at home'. The menu advertised a choice between mutton chops, pork chops or beefsteak for ten pence. This could be followed by a pot of tea for nine pence.[33] When the price of tea was almost high as the price of steak, it was indeed a luxury.

In spite of the recession Liverpool was busy, it had a population of 120,000, its 'river crowded with shipping and holds filled with cotton, corn and spice. There was a seething crowd on the waterfront, a clatter of carriages and a continual shouting as cargoes were unloaded onto the wharves. The taverns were full, the narrow streets thick with a jostling throng'.[34] Like Thomas Ripley, other merchants were moving to Liverpool with the same idea. In 1819 Thomas Brocklebank arrived from Whitehaven.[35] The Brocklebanks were to become very prominent merchants who founded a hugely successful shipping line, which lasted into the twentieth century.

Newly arrived merchants 'must have listened to the talk of

street, wharf and coffee house. Fortunes were being made by vessels sailing … to America and the West Indies.'[36] New markets were always being sought. Since the beginning of the century merchants in all the major ports of Britain had been seeking the abolition of the East India Company monopoly. Some progress had been made in 1813, from which time trade with the subcontinent of India was permitted. The Ripleys would soon take advantage of this and begin trading with Calcutta, but they and other merchants were greedy for more. They hoped for a change in the law that would also end the East India Company's monopoly over trade with China, but as Gibson writes 'for the moment all this was but a whisper, a rumour on the waterfront. A hope here and a gamble there.'[37]

By the early 1820s the economic climate was much improved. "The lowness of interest obtainable and the plethora of circulation fostered speculation, and speculation became rampant both in foreign and home concerns".[38] In 1823 Britain had begun making loans to foreign nations, principally to the newly recognized South American republics. Merchandise too was sent out in vast quantities. Anyone in Liverpool who could find the wherewithal joined in one enterprise or another. It was not long before Thomas Ripley had contacts in South America himself. However, his main source of income was still in trade with the West Indies. As trading conditions continued to improve, Thomas was getting bigger and better returns on his cargoes. He liked to maintain firm control over all his business dealings, even those in foreign ports, so he frequently made the voyage out to the West Indies to check up on the agents he had appointed there.[39]

Henry Ripley soon joined his brother Thomas in business in Liverpool. By 1821 they had set up as T & H Ripley and had premises at 21 Peter Lane.[40] At this time a merchant's office was still described as a 'counting house' - a picturesque and archaic term. Henry was the youngest of the Ripley brothers and the last to benefit from the bequests willed to him by his father and stepfather. With this capital Henry had begun to make money and to invest in shipping. By the time he joined Thomas, he already owned two vessels: the *Lorton*, a modest vessel of 160 tons, and the *Matilda*, even smaller at 147 tons.

The Mersey, Liverpool.
Lancashire Illustrated (1831)]

Owning their own vessels was of enormous value to T & H Ripley. They also acquired some loyal employees, like Captain Eves who was to remain a faithful servant of the Ripleys for years, and sailed many of their ships. Thomas now felt that he was in a position to take a wife.

Every Christmas Julia Reay's parents held merry parties at their comfortable home. Her father, William Reay, was practising as a doctor in a part of Liverpool known as Islington.[41] His wife Charlotte was also from a medical family. Medicine was still rooted in the Middle Ages in many ways. Primitive treatments and patent remedies abounded. Doctors continued to use leeches to purge their patients' blood, 'leech breeders' were listed in the local directories, and surgical instruments were still made by hand.

William Reay was described as a surgeon.[42] Liverpool surgeons ranged in ability from the highly qualified practitioner to the 'ignorant sawbones'.[43] Reay was an educated man, who also dabbled in merchant trade as a sideline, and it may have been as a result of this that Thomas Ripley met the Reay family, and became part of their social circle. He would have been introduced to Reay's three eldest daughters, Maria, Julia and Harriet.[44] The girls had a younger brother and sister named Charles and Lottie.[45]

Thomas Ripley was fourteen years older than Julia. He saw her as an attractive young woman with poise and maturity beyond her teenage years. For a girl of the Regency period Julia was exceptionally well educated and well read, like both her parents. William Reay had a great love of literature, which his daughter Julia shared. Reay belonged to the Liverpool Medical Library and served as a committee member.[46] He also had a large collection of books of his own on many subjects.[47] Julia had a keen interest in foreign travel, natural history, music, poetry, geography and even astronomy.

A romance developed between Tom and Julia. Liverpool was still quite compact, and so it was easily possible for courting couples to take picturesque walks into the countryside to visit the pretty villages of Wavertree and Everton. Julia loved to take long walks. At the theatre plays and pantomimes were performed, including the ever popular 'Whittington and his Cat', which ran at the theatre in Christian Street very near to Julia's home.[48] There was a vogue for 'fancy balls' at which elaborate costumes were worn. At these balls and at private dances, quadrilles were the order of the day, as the waltz had not yet become fashionable. For the most daring, it was even possible to go sea bathing near Waterloo, but men and women entered the sea separately using 'bathing machines' according to the modesty of the day.[49]

Friends and relatives on both sides may have doubted the wisdom of the match. Thomas and Julia were as different as chalk and cheese. He was a self-made man of the world who had seen a lot of life. She was just a young girl. He had grown up in a pub. Her family was bookish and extremely religious. He was chiefly interested in increasing his wealth, while her family had something of a social conscience. Thomas was not even a Liverpudlian.

In 1823 he swiftly resolved to marry Julia and obtained her parents official consent rather than wait for her to reach the age of twenty-one. They were married by licence at St. Anne's Church in the summer of 1823, a few months before Julia's nineteenth birthday.[50] They were in love, and both remained passionately in love for the rest of their lives. He would shower her with presents, and she would devote herself to the fulfilment of his schemes and visions. Different as they were, they saw in each other complementary qualities. Thomas wanted to use his new-found wealth to set himself up as a gentleman. In Julia he saw someone who would be an ideal hostess to his friends and business acquaintances. She was a great conversationalist, she was an accomplished pianist, and she loved dancing and socialising. Perhaps Thomas also perceived that in Julia he had found a woman with whom he could discuss his most cherished and secret ambitions. For her part, Julia longed for fashionable gowns, for jewellery, for expensive furniture and most of all she longed to travel, and she may have seen Thomas as someone who could enable her to fulfil some of her own aspirations.

At the time of the marriage Thomas Ripley was living in Great George Square. It was an area where other merchant families lived. The Gladstones had lived in nearby Rodney Street, and William Ewart Gladstone who would become prime minister, was born there. However, as they became richer both these families aspired to a more prestigious address. Thomas Ripley looked at new property being built on the outskirts of Liverpool.

Abercromby Square, home of Julia and Thomas Ripley.
Lancashire Illustrated (1831)

At the time of its construction Abercromby Square was described as 'the most spacious area of the kind in Liverpool, covering about three and a half acres of ground. On three sides it is enclosed by houses built in an elegant style and on a rectangular plan'. There was a garden in the centre of the square for the residents to use. It became 'the most fashionable square in Liverpool'.[51] Strange to think that back in the seventeenth century this had been a marshy area that had once been a lake. The water from the lake had been used to supply humble workmen like tanners and dyers. By 1827 Thomas and Henry had each bought themselves a prestigious house in Abercromby Square.[52]

From 1823 trade really took off for Thomas, and his fortunes began their meteoric rise. The *Lorton* arrived back in Liverpool in June, and anchored in King's Dock. She discharged a cargo of 1101 bags of coffee and 205 logs of mahogany for T & H Ripley.[53] By June the 19th she was entered for loading for a return voyage to Saint Domingo in the West Indies. Sales of goods like these were so successful that before long Thomas was wealthy enough to invest in another vessel, the *Spartan*, 237 tons, registered in his own name.[54]

Through Julia and her family, Thomas met new business acquaintances, including the Fremes, the M'Viccars, and the Naegelis.[55] Members of these families were to remain Tom and Julia's friends for the rest of their lives, as well as providing him with a network of valuable contacts in the merchant community. James Freme was one of the political supporters of William Huskisson when he stood for parliament in 1826. Joseph M'Viccar was a broker with an office in Exchange Buildings.[56] John Naegeli was also a merchant, who had been born in Switzerland.

Thomas Ripley's old mentors, the Burrow family, continued to prosper. Although still based in Lancaster they made increasing use of the Liverpool docks for their shipping. In January 1823 they advertised space for cargo on board their 'fine new brig *Thomas Burrow*' bound for the West Indies. They invited merchants to apply directly to 'Captain Dawson, on board, in Prince's Dock'.[57]

By January of 1826 T & H Ripley had acquired a vessel named the *St. Domingo*, she was sent to the West Indies under the command of their faithful employee, Captain Eves. The vessel was 208 tons; she was 'A1, coppered and copper fastened' and bound for Port-au-Prince.[58] In a few short years the Ripley brothers were to build up a small but valuable fleet of ships. By April the next year the brothers had commissioned a brig of 267 tons, which they named the *Ripley*. She was built at Tranmere, near Liverpool, by the shipbuilding firm Lomax and Wilson.[59] Thomas and Henry had a sister, Jane, who married a Lomax. The brig *Ripley* was entrusted to the reliable Captain Eves, and set sail for the Indian port of Calcutta – a new destination where the brothers were seeking to extend their trade. America was another new market for the Ripleys. The *Spartan* brought raw cotton from New Orleans, which would have been sold to one of the Lancashire mills to be woven into bolts of fabric.[60] The same vessel voyaged to Boston a few years later.[61]

The ship that was to be of supreme importance to Thomas and to Julia was bought in 1827. The *Bencoolen*, a three-masted ship of 402 tons with a standing bowsprit, was by far the largest vessel that Thomas Ripley had yet been able to afford. This brand new ship was built in Montreal, Canada, where timber was plentiful and construction costs were low. She was one hundred and thirteen feet long, and at her prow she was graced by the figurehead of a woman.[62] Her first voyage for the Ripleys was to Valparaiso in South America, where Thomas was also starting to build up trade.[63] The *Lorton*, the *Matilda*, and the *St. Domingo* plied the ports of the West Indies each year bringing the brothers handsome profits.

Henry, the richer of the two brothers, began seeking a wife. At the fancy dress ball held in Liverpool Town Hall in October 1827, the newspaper reported that Mr H. Ripley was seen dressed as 'a wood ranger to the King of Saxony'. Included in the party was a Miss Reay, one of Julia's unmarried sisters, dressed as 'a flower girl of Provence'.[64] Friends may have speculated that Henry would also find a bride in the Reay family, but it was not to be. Harriet Reay was to marry into a Cumberland family, and her sister Maria remained unwed. Henry was married in 1829; his bride, Mary Webb, came from a Staffordshire family.[65]

Always wanting to be upwardly mobile, the brothers had moved their business premises yet again by 1829. This time from Lower Castle Street to 10 Rumford Street.[66] Thomas and Henry probably still employed no more than one or two people in their office. Even the more prosperous Thomas Brocklebank, who owned a larger fleet of twenty vessels, usually copied his letters into his letter book himself.[67] Brocklebank's office was situated almost opposite, at number 7 Rumford Street, where he had a store with the office above. Brocklebank liked to cultivate contacts in the merchant community in the hope of encouraging them to send their freight in his ships. A business relationship was fostered between the Ripleys and the Brocklebanks, and for years Thomas Ripley imported some of his goods in Brocklebank bottoms.

* * *

1829 was a year of feverish agitation in Britain concerning the opening of the trade to China. The great East India Company, a vast and all-powerful organisation, had been granted a charter by Queen Elizabeth I.[68] Amongst many other things, the charter gave the company a complete monopoly over Britain's trade with China. This meant that all the tea drunk in England was imported

18

by the East India Company (EIC), because until the 1840s China was the only place where tea was grown for export.[69] So private merchants were frustrated that they could not get a share of the enormous profits that the tea trade offered. Consumers were frustrated by the high prices that had to be paid for tea. In the North of England, this was even more of a problem because the EIC's ships only used the port of London. Cargoes of tea had to be transhipped to other areas, inflating the costs again. There was 100% duty on tea at that time; it provided one-tenth of the total revenue of England.[70] The EIC charter was due for another renewal in 1833.

Shipping in the Mersey.
Lancashire Illustrated (1831)

Early in January 1829 Liverpool merchants were clamouring for free trade with China. "The one object desired by friends of free trade was that the legislature would refuse the next application of the EIC for the renewal of their charter."[71] To rally support for the merchants' cause pamphlets advocating free trade were distributed. A committee called the East India Association had already been set up to look into the restrictions placed on the China trade, with a view to reform.[72] It joined forces with a similar committee based in Manchester to add weight to their campaign. They lobbied the MP for Liverpool, William Huskisson, who urged them to seek more publicity.

At a public meeting in the courtroom, Liverpool, one of the Gladstones' spoke of the huge importance of the trade to China, arguing that "it would furnish a greatly extended market for our productions, *[and]* it would enable us to import the productions of China for our own consumption."[73] The market was hungry for greater quantities of tea and Chinese silk, especially since the duty on silk had been reduced in 1825. It was unanimously resolved at the meeting that the opening of free trade to China would be "of incalculable benefit".

In a letter to the *Liverpool Times* a vehement protest was made: "the Charter of the EIC is like a millstone round the neck of this country paralysing the efforts of merchant *[and]* shipowner".[74] Although the EIC had enjoyed its monopoly for more than two centuries, *this time* merchants felt there was at last some hope that the monopoly would be ended.

Seized with wild optimism that they would get the changes that they wanted, some merchants began to plan voyages to China. By 1830 the shipowner Brocklebank, for example, had already made plans to send his ships there.[75] Thomas Ripley also wanted to be among the first merchants to engage in free trade with China. If the monopoly *was* about to end, he wanted to be poised to take advantage of this exciting new opportunity. He felt that nothing short of a personal visit to China would suffice. He started to make ready for a voyage to the Far East. This was a most daring undertaking. The round trip would last for nearly two years, so

Thomas had to make it pay. At various ports en route he could engage in legitimate trade, but the cargo he took to China would have to be smuggled in, as China was not open to free trade.[76] Thomas Ripley was prepared to defy the edicts of the Emperor of China.

Naturally, when planning the voyage, Thomas chose the *Bencoolen*, his largest and newest vessel. He negotiated a deal on a cargo of cotton piece goods from Manchester. He accepted bookings from paying passengers. In the 1830s there was no passenger service to Asia, but many cargo vessels had a few steerage cabins available to passengers at an exorbitant price. Three passengers arranged to travel on the Bencoolen. They were Mr. Watson, Mr. Roe, and a friend of Tom's who was always referred to as 'the Doctor'.[77]

It took months to sail to the Far East, so Thomas planned to visit Batavia (now known as Jakarta), Singapore, Manila, and most importantly Macao. From Macao it was just a short distance up the River Bogue to the notorious open shipping roads of Lintin. Lintin was the centre of operations for the illicit smuggling of the drug opium into China.[78] Other goods such as rice and saltpetre were also smuggled into China through Lintin. The smuggling occurred because the Chinese put a quota on all imports. British vessels using Lintin were referred to as 'free traders'. This use of Lintin island for smuggling opium would lead directly to war between Britain and China.

Faced with the prospect of being at sea for over a year, Thomas found that he could not bear to be parted from his young wife for so long. He decided to take Julia with him. It was an unconventional decision, to take a woman on a perilous adventure to a part of the world he had never seen before. She planned to document all her experiences in a diary that she called her journal, so that she would have a record of the voyage of a lifetime. A small leather-bound book with blank pages was bought from John Ormandy's Bookseller and Stationer in Church Street. [79] The empty pages were soon to be filled with all the details of Thomas and Julia's travel adventures. It would also give glimpses of the lives of the seamen and the hardships they endured, as well as the pranks they enjoyed.

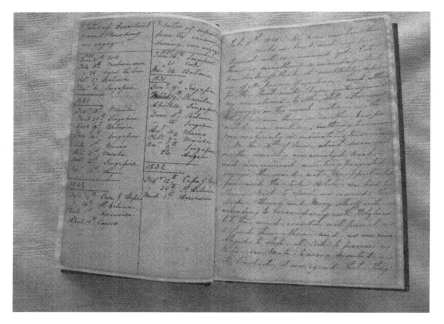

The first page of Julia Ripley's Diary

By May 1830, the *Bencoolen* was entered for loading. Her destination was given as Batavia, now known as Jakarta.[80] Obviously no mention could be made of their ultimate destination – the smuggler's island of Lintin, China. Thomas exerted himself to the utmost in making his ship ready for sea. Captain and crew had to be signed on. Cargo had to be bought and loaded onto the vessel. The cargo consisted of many thousands of yards of cotton fabric from the mills in Manchester. There were cambrics, twills, and printed cottons, as well as quantities of woollen cloth, worsted stuffs and linens.[81] At this time, merchants sometimes still shouldered the whole cost of cargoes themselves, but more often received financial backing from their agents. Exports were essential to the success of the new factories in the North of England, hence Liverpool merchants like Thomas Ripley played a key role in the Industrial Revolution.

For the long sea voyage, cabins had to be fitted out and furnished for the Ripleys' personal use. Contemporary recommendations suggested that cabins should contain the following items: a sleeping couch with drawers and a chintz cover, a horsehair sofa, and swinging cots for rough weather.[82] The Ripleys' invested in a pair of cots linked together, which they called 'our fiddle case'. The list continued with a mahogany table containing a washstand, a mahogany swinging table, a chest of drawers, a portable patent water closet, a looking-glass, candlesticks, a book rack, carpets or mats for the cabin, port and door curtains, and a foot tub. It was considered a wise precaution to take a medicine chest 'fitted up' and a filtering stone. For dining, silver spoons, forks, teacups, plates and glasses were required. These elegant pieces of tableware were juxtaposed with more mundane items such as a quart tin jug, tea kettle and corkscrew.[83] We know from the Ripley diary that Julia's cabins did contain many of these things as she refers to them often.

Travelling light was not recommended in 1830, quite the contrary. Ladies were expected to change their voluminous underclothing every day. Since there were no facilities for laundering these clothes on board ship women normally took as many changes of underclothing as the number of days they expected the voyage to last.[84] On a long sea voyage the climate changed several times, so travellers were advised to take a whole assortment of underwear, including cambric slips, long cloth petticoats, flannel petticoats, day chemises, night chemises, nightcaps, dressing gowns, flannel gowns, and quantities of pairs of cambric drawers. Accessories included muslin and silk handkerchiefs for the neck, numerous pairs of cotton and silk hose in white and black, gloves of cotton and kid, dress shoes, walking shoes and boots. Outer garments might include coloured morning dresses – black silk was especially recommended for the voyage – as well as dinner dresses, white or fancy evening dresses, shawls, a silk cloak, leghorn bonnets, parasol, and an assortment of millinery.

Young woman in a fashionable dress, circa 1830

It was not the custom to possess such huge quantities of clothing for normal use. Middle class women usually owned just a fraction of this extensive wardrobe, so most of this had to be bought or made especially for the voyage. The purchase of such things would have taken up a lot of Julia's time in the weeks before the voyage. Then she would have supervised her maids as they packed them into trunks ready to be taken on board.

Tom had been on many voyages before so he would have had firm views on what should be packed for him. Gentlemen were advised to take plenty of white jean or sateen trousers, 'knapt coating coats', coloured trousers, Irish or Scotch linen trousers, Russia drill trousers, Musquetto trousers, camlet jackets or coatees made of jean, silk, or superfine cloth, with matching waistcoats. Undergarments for men included white or black hose made of silk, cotton or worsted. Men also needed a store of leather or cotton gloves, braces, long cloth shirts, nightshirts, neck handkerchiefs, leather stocks and extra collars.[85]

Bed linen was also required for the voyage, including a hair mattress, a bolster, and mosquito curtains. Table linen included dozens of napkins and tablecloths. For her personal use, Julia would have needed a dressing case for her perfume, cologne water, and combs, a workbox 'furnished with a complete assortment of haberdashery', a pocket-knife and scissors, and a writing desk with stationery.

Julia also decided that her maid, Catherine, was indispensable. She needed someone to help her dress, to look after her on the voyage and for female companionship. Catherine had to pack for herself as well as for her mistress. As a servant, Catherine would have travelled with a much more modest quantity of clothing.

The diary tells us that the Ripleys' cook prepared some

preserved food for them to take on their voyage. This included eggs and preserved salmon.[86] She may have also made other contemporary delicacies like raspberry vinegar, currant jelly, and biscuits which travellers were advised to take. It was also possible to buy ready prepared hermetically sealed food. But at twelve shillings and sixpence for a jar of preserved turtle, this was an extravagant purchase.[87] Travellers were told to pack pounds of tea, coffee, sugar, and a supply of drinking chocolate, to enjoy on board ship. They would need pounds of wax candles, Windsor and Castile Soap, which could be stored in cases lined with tin.

Julia decided to take a small piano as a source of musical entertainment. It was duly hoisted on board ship. Livestock such as pigs and ducks were penned up on deck in cages to supply the Ripleys and the passengers with fresh meat from time to time.

While these elaborate preparations were being made on board the *Bencoolen*, another ship was entered for loading for Batavia. She was the *Meredith*, under Captain Fullerton. The two ships were similar in size and tonnage. Thomas Ripley was convinced that his ship was faster even though she was more heavily laden. Fullerton thought that by pushing the *Meredith* to her limits he was in with a chance of reaching Batavia first. A race was set up and wagers were most likely made.

At the last minute, Henry Ripley announced that he too would take advantage of the earliest part of the voyage in order to visit Holyhead. His wife Mary was to accompany him.

On the brink of departure, the ship was threatened with delay. It was discovered that the First Mate had deserted. His decision not to sail with the *Bencoolen* is a very telling one. He was second only to the Captain, and he would have had lots of extra privileges over and above the rest of the crew. We know that Captain Roberts was not a harsh man, so it looks as if the First

Mate could not tolerate working alongside the ship's owner, Thomas Ripley. Often an impatient man, Thomas decided that he wouldn't wait to look for a suitable replacement in Liverpool. The ship set sail as planned.

Julia takes up the story in her journal.

A Liverpool steam tug.
Lancashire Illustrated (1831)

The Ripley Diary

3

Aboard the Good Ship *Bencoolen*

Perch Rock lighthouse, built on Black Rock.
Lancashire Illustrated (1831)

On the 16th of June about seven o'clock in the evening we weighed anchor and commenced our long projected voyage. The wind not being particularly fair and the tide so late we had a steamboat to assist us round the Rock. Henry and Mary set off with us, intending to accompany us to Holyhead but the wind would not permit us to land them there and as we were obliged to stop at Cork to procure a mate (our mate having deserted us at Liverpool) it was agreed that they should also proceed to Cork.

Sunday June 20th A most beautiful day not a cloud to be seen, and the sea quite smooth – soon after breakfast a steamboat was seen which upon approaching the ship proved to be the *Herald* from Cork to Liverpool. Henry most unexpectedly took a whim into his head to return by her very much to the disappointment of his wife who as she had been obliged to make so much longer sea voyage than she expected or liked had consoled herself by the anticipation of returning through the most beautiful and romantic scenery of Ireland besides seeing some of the principal cities – Cork, Dublin, etc. But Henry was resolved and wives must obey. About 11 o'clock they quitted us, Tom and the Captain accompanying them on board. I felt very great regret at parting with them.

June 21st About five in the morning the Captain came down to awake Tom to tell him Cork was in sight at last and a pilot on board. Tom and the Doctor accordingly rose, got a little breakfast and went on shore in search of a mate. Poor Mary! I pitied her very much, the weather had completely changed since the preceding day and it was blowing very strongly in our favour consequently quite contrary for the Herald. I fear they would have a very bad passage and Mary would suffer much. I was very ill all day and obliged to remain in bed where I scrawled a few lines to my dear mother. At five in the evening the gentleman returned having been very successful in procuring an efficient mate, a man who had been a master of vessels for the last fourteen years. The Doctor made many useful purchases and very kindly thought of me and brought me some fine strawberries and prawns, but I was not sufficiently well to enjoy them. *[Julia was suffering from seasickness.]* They had taken the empty water casks on shore intending to get them filled, water being such a valuable commodity, but the day was so stormy it was not considered safe to take them filled in the boat. As soon as possible after their return, we sailed. Again the wind being fair, but it did not continue in our favour many hours.

June 24th – Ventured on deck for the first time since Sunday, a very fine day but the wind still unfavourable, making scarcely any progress. Saw a great number of porpoises playing about the ship. Dined on deck.

June 26th – The day so calm and fine that I ventured for the first time since coming on board to join the gentlemen at dinner and went through the ceremony admirably well. The evening became very stormy and it continued to blow hard during the night, so much that we had a pretty rough specimen of the famous Bay of Biscay – O. I was not sufficiently inured to the sea to sleep through it very soundly, and although we had taken the precaution of having everything secured and after shipping a little water had the deadlights put in, still the noises were incessant and kept us the whole night upon the qui vive. We also found it necessary in consequence of the rolling of the vessel to follow the example of the old man 'n' his wife and have recourse to our fiddle case – not from the same cause. *[This is the first of many veiled references to Thomas and Julia's healthy sex life!]*

June 27th – The wind much abated but the sea very high in consequence of the storm. Obliged to remain in bed although able to eat a tolerable breakfast and dinner so that my situation was not so very deplorable. Lost one of our poor pigeons, I suppose it must have flown from the ship and the wind was too strong for it to return, we now have only three left out of the six but they are become exceedingly tame and domesticated.

June 30th – Tom came down with the delightful intelligence that the wind at last had determined to befriend us, a most agreeable resolution after tantalising us for fourteen days. Dined again in the dining room and continued it for the future. Judged prudent to commence an allowance of water in case of a long voyage – five pints a day each. *[The imprudent decision not to wait and take on adequate supplies of water at Cork was the start of the deterioration of owner-crew relations which was to have serious repercussions. It was aggravating for the crew to endure water rationing when there could have been plenty.]* Tom very busy for several days trying to produce good leaven in which he succeeded, we have now nice hot rolls every morning to breakfast.

Sunday July 4th – Wind still very favourable. A party to dinner consisting of three steerage passengers and the Second Mate. Made trial of the salmon and found it as good as represented. The soups also are excellent … *[The second mate, Mr. Carr, may have envied the luxury foods the Ripleys consumed each day. Enjoying the rare privilege of dining with his employers, Carr may have reflected on the fact that the food they gave the crew was inadequate to maintain good health. The crew had none of the fine things he saw at the Ripleys' table. Significantly, it was Carr who lead the mutiny later in the voyage.]*

July 5th – About two o'clock in the morning the Captain came down to say that Madeira could be seen, a very joyful hearing after being nineteen days in accomplishing such a small portion of our voyage. Tom arose and went on deck where we found the Doctor, Catherine, and all assembled, but as I expected I should be something in Catherine's way and not able to see it, I did not think it worthwhile to take the trouble of dressing at that time of night as it only appeared like a black cloud. Several flying fish seen but I was not fortunate enough to be on deck.

We have a most incorrigible little fellow on board, Frank Brown, an American; according to his own account, which by the by, is not always to be depended upon, he was enticed from his native place, Philadelphia, by a smuggler, when he was about ten years of age. He landed at Milford and was so little satisfied with his situation that he ran away, and found his way by some means to Liverpool. We hear all kinds of complaints against him, but today he was in great disgrace having been detected feasting upon some sugar belonging to one of the men, and what he could not eat he deposited in the coal hole until a more 'convenient season'. He got so well punished for it that to alarm the people he ran to the side of the vessel and threatened to jump overboard, but that is a catastrophe we do not need to fear, the Mate says he is too great a rogue for that, he will live to be king. Be that as it may he vows the first land he can put his feet upon, be it in whatever part of the world it may, he will bid adieu to the good ship Bencoolen. *[The ship's boy Frank Brown probably was telling the truth when he claimed to have been press-ganged at Philadelphia. Vessels calling at American ports frequently lost members of their crew, who jumped ship to start a new life there]*

July 9th – Tom arose about seven to look what kind of a morning it was, he suddenly exclaimed "My dear, look here, look here!"

I rose immediately not being able to imagine what could possibly have excited his astonishment so strongly when low 'n' behold, there was a large ship, in full sail, not more than a mile from us – we spoke her and found her to be the *Roxborough Castle* from London bound to Calcutta – enquired after the King, and learned that he was very bad. A number of troops on board which as clearly as we could understand were the Fourteenth Dragoons but we could not hear distinctly. There appeared to be several ladies, no doubt the officers' wives. Requested them to report us to the first vessel they meet and also at Calcutta. They sailed seven days after us but she was considerably lighter and consequently in much better condition for despatch besides which she is a remarkably fast sailer and indeed has never been known to make a long passage which very much inspirits Tom, he thinks as we follow her so immediately we quite ensure a good voyage to Batavia. It is surprising what a great degree of interest an incident of this kind creates at sea. It furnishes fresh topics of conversation for several days.

...Begin to feel the delights of a tropical climate although hitherto we have had a nice breeze which has prevented the heat being very intolerable. When I was sitting on deck with my work the Captain exclaimed "Mrs. Ripley, there is a Portuguese Man of War!"

I jumped up, expecting of course to see a fine warlike looking ship, I strained my eyes in vain, I could see nothing – but some time after standing looking over the side of the vessel Tom pointed out to me a small white substance which I should have fancied a piece of chip, this was a Portuguese Man of War. I should imagine it to be something of the same nature as the jellyfish. They have a very luminous appearance at night, on a dark night the sea looks most beautiful. I suppose it is little animalculae which become so illuminated that the ship sometimes appears almost to be going through fire.

July 11th - A party to dinner – a vessel descried in the morning gaining upon us very quickly. After dinner hailed. She proved to be the *Thomas Battersby* from Liverpool bound to Pernambuco. Requested the Captain to take letters for us to that port and send them to England by the first good opportunity, which he agreed to do.

All hastened down to prepare despatches, which required little more than directing and sealing. The jolly boat lowered and the Doctor sent in charge of the budget. He returned with very little news except that the King continued very ill, almost exhausted – a state to which my patience is almost reduced to, to see us so much beaten, but we cannot avoid it, we are so deeply laden. The *Thomas Battersby* was in ballast. The Captain bid us goodbye expecting soon to distance us, but we did not lose sight of the vessel until the following evening. It will be three months before our friends in Liverpool will receive our letters but we have duplicates prepared for any vessel we may meet homeward bound.

[These enquiries about the health of George IV sound solicitous of his welfare, but in fact many people in England were tired of the excesses of the King. Merchants especially hoped his successor would favour free trade. Little did the Ripleys know that George IV had died just after the Thomas Battersby set sail. They had no way of knowing the latest news that William IV had become the new King on 26 June.]

July 12th - A prodigious commotion in the evening. Lat. 16 – 16. The vicinity of the Cape Verde islands. Came down about seven and prepared tea, waited a long time for Tom, when he came he said there was a light seen ahead which they could not make out unless it proceeded from the *Thomas Battersby*. Upon going upon deck after tea, it presented a most singular appearance – everyone on board trying to conjecture what it could possibly be. The Captain thought it a phenomenon in the heavens. One man called it Jack o' the lantern, one will o' the wisp, some thought as we were in a bad neighbourhood, it might be a pirate vessel, adopting that way of enticing us to see what it was. This idea struck me as being a very probable one, but the blaze at intervals was so exceedingly vivid that all (except the Captain who persisted in his original opinion) thought it not impossible it might be a vessel on fire, or making signals of distress. This idea, once suggested, everybody was anxious to approach it to ascertain more distinctly what it really was, or if we could render any assistance. The Captain, however, refused, saying we should most probably only be running into danger, until Tom insisted upon it, urging that it would be the height of cruelty to have the most distant idea of its being a ship in distress and not to go out of our way a few miles to give assistance. And if it should be a pirate, we had a fine ship, well armed and plenty of men to use the arms, what had we to fear? Accordingly, all hands were set to make preparations for defence against an enemy. The bosun got ready the great guns, the arms chest was unlocked – muskets, swords, handspikes, pistols, all in demand. The Doctor and Tom fetched their pistols, and thus prepared we made towards the object, which had occasioned so much excitement. In half an hour we had approached sufficiently near to ascertain that it was a vessel very brilliantly lighted, but for what purposes we still (and ever must) remain in ignorance. It was agreed *nem con* that it bore a very suspicious appearance, and that it would not be prudent to go any nearer. Accordingly, we retraced our track again, but continued on the watch as it was imagined that the other ship had now changed her course also, and would very soon cross our stern.

"I would advise you ma'am," says the steward, "to go down into the cabin, for when they come near enough they will fire a great gun into us, and it is impossible to say what the consequences may be."

However, no such catastrophe happened, and we found ourselves gradually leaving them behind us. We felt great satisfaction in being convinced that we had left no fellow creatures in distress when it was in our power to afford them the least assistance. The light continued visible for a length of time, but between eleven and twelve we thought we might venture to bed, and arose in the morning all safe and well, and so ended our adventure, which produced one good effect, that of having our guns prepared, which had not previously been attended to.

July 14th – All very busy and much amused trying to catch fish, with which the sea today seemed actually alive, of a description called albacore, which feed upon the beautiful little flying fish. It was really a pretty sight to watch the chase. The flying fish arose in immense flocks and continued so long above the water that I had for the first time a very good opportunity of distinguishing what they were like. Previously they had been much smaller and seemed to me so like the spray that I could not discern them from it. The albacores pursued them with great spirit, and sometimes I am sure leapt at least six or eight feet out of the water after them. The Doctor compared them to a pack of hounds after poor puss, rather an apt comparison I think.

Every means was tried to make a prize of some of the enemy, and according to the opinion of some anglers I may say they had a good day's sport, for they had three actual bites, by which they lost as many hooks. Two were carried away in toto, and one broken in attempting to secure the tempting bait by which Tom had endeavoured to seduce them. I must confess he had displayed great ingenuity and had succeeded in making a few very handsome flying fish. I do not know whether I shall be liable to consequences for publishing his secret to the world, but I will run the risk. With part of a spermacite candle he formed the body of the fish, upon this for the back, he fastened a piece of black ribbon and two small hens feathers for the wings, and put two tacks in the head for eyes, and really the deception was very good, but the foe was too powerful, indeed the gentlemen imagine them to be a fish weighing from one to three cwt. To me they did not appear more than sixty or eighty pounds, but anything seen underwater has a very deceptive look. The hooks and lines proving so inefficient, and the gentlemen feeling so anxious to heave one on board, one of the men was sent into the jollyboat to try the grain, but the fish were too expert to allow him an opportunity of displaying his dexterity, and as a last resource, the Doctor and Tom armed themselves with guns for the contest, but after giving a few unsuccessful shots, the fish were declared victorious.

The seventh anniversary of our wedding day – one apprenticeship served. God Almighty grant that we may be spared many years to enjoy health and happiness equal to the last seven … We had a bottle of champagne on the occasion and in the evening the men had an extra glass of grog, and I received all their thanks and congratulations.

4

The Atlantic Ocean: A Race Between Two Rival Ships

July 15th – the poor Doctor rose this morning with one of his eyes very much inflamed and painful, and appeared very uneasy about it, never having had anything the matter with his eyes before. He could not tell to what to attribute it, unless it was the heat, or the sea air, but we discovered the cause and not withstanding the Doctor's suffering could not help enjoying a hearty laugh at his expense. It seems he had been visited by some bed fellows, which very much annoyed him, and the Captain recommended him to put some pepper in his bed as an antidote, meaning peppercorns, but the doctor got the cruets from the castors and sprinkled his mattress almost as thick of pepper as dust on a macadam road in a dry season. When the searching nature of pepper is considered it is not very surprising that after tossing about upon it for a whole night he should have awoke in the morning with his eyes inflamed.

[The problem of dust on macadam roads was only later to be solved by the invention of tar macadam, which we know as

38

tarmac.]

July 16th – Today we have entered upon a part of our passage dominated by the variables of the great changeableness of the weather in climate. Our latitude today about 8-50- north. The Captain gives us a very unprepossessing description of the weather we are likely to have until we approach within two or three degrees of the equator. He says the wind frequently veers all round the compass and there is thunder and lightening, rain and sunshine, all in the space of a very short time. Sometimes vessels are detained a long time within a few degrees of the equator, and sometimes they go directly through the variables, which I hope will be our case, and that we shall not find them so terrible as the Captain describes.

We had some delightful rain this afternoon, which created quite a bustle on board – the first we have had for at least three *[weeks?]*. Tom was very busy teaching the people the best method of catching the water, which is a most valuable commodity on a long sea voyage. With a little good management they succeeded in securing four or five days supply. The sailors made a complete washing day of it, and I was amused to see how gay the ship looked bedecked with red and blue shirts, etc. We had such a grunting and gabbling and quacking – all the pigs and geese and ducks were set at liberty to enjoy the full benefit of the shower and wash and clean themselves, it did them, as the country people say, a power of good, and so improved their appearance that I am sure I shall partake of the next that grace the dinner table with increased *goût [good appetite]*.

I forgot to mention that about ten I made a very successful attempt at cooking a preserved tart and dish of cheesecakes, which were pronounced excellent.

July 18th – About five o'clock in the morning the Captain

came down and said, "There is a large ship in sight, sir."

"Which way is she bound?"

"The same way as ourselves."

The usual answer. I begin to despair of ever meeting with a vessel bound direct for England. I fear my dear parents will suffer great anxiety before they can possibly receive any tidings from us. They will I know imagine that we have neglected opportunity of which we might have taken advantage. I wish I could make them aware how impatient we are of forwarding intelligence of ourselves and our little community. The vessel we saw (... like several others we have seen) left us in the distance, *[it]* was an American South Sea whaler, and proved a means of depriving us of two of our prime pets *[pigeons]*–Today they took their usual airing, but melancholy to relate, two out of the three never returned, and as the day was very fine we can only account for their absence by supposing they mistook the Yankee for their own home ...

A flying fish was found on board this morning, it had no doubt made an extra exertion to avoid one of the numerous enemies by which these poor little creatures are tormented, and by doing so had rushed into an evil equally fatal. I was glad of an opportunity of examining one for I could not in their short and hasty flights upon the water distinguish what they were like. It was a small specimen that I saw, but a beautiful little fish, in colour like a mackerel, but not at all in form, and not larger than a small sized sparling *[a young herring]* – the wings of a very gauze-like texture. I should think it must be a very delicate eating fish, I hope I shall have an opportunity of tasting it before we return again.

Flying Fish.

We begin to feel very sensibly that we are in a tropical climate, we have not yet fortunately suffered from what sailors so much dread, a calm, and having a nice breeze and during the day our awning spread over the deck to keep off the sun, the day is tolerably pleasant, not hotter than a fine summer's day in England – the thermometer not having reached higher than eighty degrees in the shade. But I dread the approach of night, the air seems to become insupportably oppressive – I cannot account for it, but it certainly is a fact, it is quite an antidote to sleep, at least we find it so, but we understand from the Captain that he still uses <u>three blankets and a counterpane</u>, whilst we cannot endure any bed covering at all. I cannot conceive what materials he can possibly be made of; he must at any rate have a fine East Indian constitution.

Contrary wind and rather rough, the vessel pitching and tossing so much that it prevented me joining the usual Sunday dinner party. I dined on deck.

July 21st – A very unusual occurrence took place today about breakfast time, a ship was descried astern, which the captain declared very like the *Meredith*, our famous opponent, but we all fancied she must have distanced us completely in consequence of our having been obliged to stop at Cork, and also her great advantage over us in being so much lighter. However, when she made her number to the surprise of everyone on board, she really proved to be the *Meredith*. We brought to and held a long conversation with the captain *[the Meredith's captain's name was Fullerton]*, which ended by our inviting him to dine with us at three o'clock. He accepted our invitation and at the appointed hour we despatched our jollyboat for him. He spent two or three hours with us, and then returned and the two rivals commenced their race again upon fair terms. Instances of this kind do sometimes occur, but they are very rare, and it certainly is remarkable that two vessels leaving the same port at the same time and bound to the same place should fall in with each other upon such an immense expanse of water as we now are.

The weather became a little more favourable today although we may consider ourselves particularly fortunate in our run through the variables. We lost the northeast trade winds on the 16th but though the wind was rather contrary the weather was fine. We had neither much rain, nor any thunder, nor lightening, as we were led to expect. But today there is every appearance of the southeast trade and Tom is in great spirits about it.

July 22nd – lat. 4. 15 N Long. 16. 55 W. The wind today declared a regular trade wind a most delightful day, and the air much less oppressive than we have experienced it for the last week.

The night was one of the loveliest I ever remember seeing. The day closed with a splendid sunset, indeed each day our admiration is called forth by the magnificent sunsets, they differ every evening but we find it very difficult to decide which have exhibited the greatest degree of grandeur. The days now close a little after six. We have a new moon and as soon as one luminary takes leave the other makes its appearance, it was exceedingly brilliant this evening, and gives every indication of continuance of fine weather. At ten o'clock at night I joined Tom on deck to enjoy the beauty of the scene. The luminosity of the sea was very fine. Tom says he never saw anything to equal it in any of his numerous voyages to the West Indies ....

I had been reading the 107th psalm in the morning, the proper psalm for the day, and was much struck with the latter part where David describes how particularly God makes his power known at sea. It begins, "They that go down to the sea in ships, and occupy their business in great waters, these men see the works of the Lord, and His wonders in the deep."

In the morning, our foretopmast was discovered to have sprung, but as we have had no bad weather, Tom thinks it must have been before we left.

My poor piano is a very great invalid, it suffers severely from the effects of climate, and neither my spouse nor I prove very skilful physicians. I fear it will be of little or no use to me now, I regret it because I enjoyed it very much whilst it remained in tune, and had intended to have returned to England quite a proficient. However I am not afraid of wanting employment, or even for a moment suffering the least degree of ennui. Indeed I have not yet found time to commence perfecting myself in French. As to Spanish, I have quite given up the idea of studying it without instruction. I think it is almost better not to learn a language than to learn it badly and acquire incorrect and inelegant pronunciation, which I should certainly do if I attempted to teach myself Spanish, and to confess the truth I have no talent as a linguist.

July 24th – The appearance of the sea was singularly beautiful tonight, we have seen nothing like it before ... the luminous substances seemed to be below the surface of the water and of such a size and brilliancy that they really excited our astonishment. We called for one of the men to fish for us and were surprised upon a nearer view to find they were substances at least two inches long and the circumference of a man's thumb, and by keeping them in constant motion, retained their shining properties. The little sparklers we have seen before were very bright, but when out of the water would have required a microscope to discern them accurately. I examined our encyclopaedia to find an account of them, but it is upon too small a scale to give any detailed description ... I shall certainly endeavour to obtain some elucidation upon the subject, if I live to return to England. *[The information Julia was seeking was not available in 1830, the luminescence was caused by small electric currents that the sea creatures generated as they moved.]*

July 25th – Today at about five o'clock pm, we crossed the line, and about eight it was announced to the Captain that Neptune's boat was approaching the ship. He held a short conversation with his Majesty, who declared his intention (as the day was so far advanced) of renewing his visit next morning to receive his tithes. That he had merely called today to inquire after his children for whom he feels great anxiety. The colloquy being ended he departed in his chariot of fire in the form of a tar barrel and we were amused at watching it rise and sink with the undulation of the water until we receded so far from each other that it appeared almost like a star in the distance.

[When a ship 'crossed the line' or the equator, the crew were usually given permission to celebrate in the traditional way. The seamen would pose as Neptune and his attendants and play various practical jokes on those who had not been across the line before.]

Walking the Plank.

July 26th – This morning we were obliged to rise an hour earlier than usual, a little after seven, in order to make preparations for the reception of 'our illustrious stranger', he having declared it his intention to be on board at eight o'clock. But like all people of distinction, to show his consequence I suppose, he was not at all punctual. It was nearly ten o'clock when we received a message to say that Neptune had arrived and desired the pleasure of our company on deck. We immediately attended the summons, and I was not a little amused at the scenes that ensued. His Majesty was accompanied by his goddess, and a numerous train of tritons. A more grotesque group I certainly never saw. They looked just like a set of mountebanks from some country fair. They were covered all over with rags and jags and feathers, and daubed with red and black. After making enquiries about our health and very politely presenting me with some fish, fresh caught in the morning, very much resembling dried herrings, Neptune gave us to understand that his employment for the day would be of such a laborious nature that it was necessary for him to commence operations .... By far the greater part of the company were strangers in his domains and that he should levy contributions upon <u>all</u> without any distinction of rank or person, except for the lady. Those who did not choose to pay the tax must take the consequences. Even Catherine was obliged to bribe this corrupt Monarch. All the condemned persons had been kept in close custody during the morning while the preparations for 'shaving' were going forward, that they might not be aware what a treat awaited them. When this list was produced, it appeared that the gentlemen were enrolled first, but they very soon made their peace by promising a liberal bonus.

Next came the steerage passengers who we quite expected they would have allowed to escape, being very respectable men, but as the mate says

"Sailors are no respecters of persons on these occasions".

And so it proved, for the first led to the place of execution was Mr. Watson a Scotchman, and a very Sir Pertinaxish sort of gentleman, who himself had never calculated upon going through the ordeal.[88] However he was blindfolded and led forward and after mounting a few steps, was seated upon the edge of a sail, rigged and filled with water for the occasion, the barber being in readiness, with his can of tar for soap, and a piece of an old iron hoop for a razor. Neptune then began to interrogate him, but receiving no answer he desired the barber to do his duty. Woe betide the man that fall into the hands of such tonsure. I was excessively entertained with watching the proceedings. The poor fellow got plentifully lathered with the tar mixture and as well scraped with the razor, and during the operation, fearful that he might feel faint, he was refreshed with a little wine, not the most agreeable beverage in the world, and to conclude the ceremony he was pushed backwards into the sail full of water and there were plenty of bystanders ready to throw buckets of water upon him, so that he got a complete ducking. All the rest in turn went through the same ceremony, some less courageously than others, especially the poor joiner, who I believe really thought when he got into the water that he was actually overboard. Catherine did not quite escape, for after they had finished shaving, one of them came very unexpectedly and threw a bucket of water over her, it completely offended her dignity and she very foolishly spent the greater part of the day in weeping over it. The Captain, Doctor and Tom took care to remain in the cabin for some time; otherwise they would have shared the same fate. I was the only person who dared look upon the proceedings with impunity. The rest of the day was spent by the men in drinking and amusing themselves and I really believe they would be glad to receive a visit from Neptune every day, notwithstanding his severe treatment. We gave them a fine mess of soup and boulli with green peas and gravy to add to it, and ordered them a plum pudding so that they had holiday fare.

July 31st ... for the last two days the men have been busily engaged taking down the foretopmast which was in a defective and dangerous state, and replacing it with a new one. We had rather a high sea today, which treated me very ungallantly. I was sitting very industriously and intently working when to my great astonishment a Sea came and soused me completely. It was so unexpected that I had no time to elude its effect. I could not help thinking how my Liverpool friends would have laughed at me if they had seen me like that; "Wild youth Genius, dripping from the current".[89] It is not the first time that I have been christened with water from the "Briny Ocean", and I shall have reason to consider myself very fortunate if I do not receive any more severe visitations than I have hitherto experienced.

A vessel seen today and at length declared to be <u>homeward bound</u>. We spoke her and to our great delight she proved to be going direct to Liverpool: the *Lord Byron* from Montevideo. We immediately prepared our despatches, which in nearly seven weeks had swelled to a very respectable size, notwithstanding the scarcity of incident in a sea life. Tom went on board to deliver them to the captain and took him a Liverpool paper thinking it would be a great treat to him, but he seemed very indifferent about news. I cannot express how much I felt relieved and delighted at so favourable an opportunity of sending home letters. What gratification they will afford! I almost began to despair of meeting a homeward bound ship, I really did not like the idea of our friends supposing we had forgotten or neglected them – as it is I fear before they receive our despatches we shall have fallen under the lash of their displeasure. God grant the letters may find them all in health and happiness!

Some dolphin seen today and various kinds of bait thrown out to seduce them, but they were proof against temptation. It is rather singular that they are the first we have seen during our voyage.

Our last poor pigeon disappeared today; its fate however is unfortunately unsolved in great obscurity. We cannot tell whether it deserted to the *Lord Byron*, whether in a fit of melancholy it committed suicide, or whether, which is most probable it became prey to one of the greedy and ravenous little pigs with each a fowl in its mouth. I cannot say that its disappearance affected me very seriously, for since the loss of its companions, it has been really an object of pity.

August 5th – Today we were almost becalmed, indeed in the evening I may say quite so. When sitting at my work in the morning, Tom called to me from the deck.

"My dear, my dear, a whale!"

The cry went round,

"Doctor, a whale!"

We hastened above and really saw something very like a whale, *[and soon more whales were sighted]* … and upon referring to the encyclopaedia we found they were a species of whale *[called fin whales]*, …having a fin near to the tale. We saw them rise above the water and blow several times. One of them appeared to be a 'huge leviathan', although partially as it was seen, it was impossible to form a correct idea of its size. I am very glad that I have seen these wonders of the deep, it has been my chief anxiety during our voyage, and I almost began to fear my curiosity would not be gratified. But the men say if we live to reach the Cape we shall see plenty. We are illuminated now by the most beautiful moon I ever saw; the nights are literally as clear as the day. I do not think it is imagination alone which induces me to say I never saw it so bright in England. The freedom from smoke and impurity in the atmosphere may easily account for its greater brilliance. Tom enjoys his nocturnal rambles particularly and often wishes he had his friend Mr. Naegeli to accompany him. He thinks he would so much relish his moonlight walks, a cigar, and a bottle of porter.

August 6th – 'After a storm comes a calm', and I suppose vice versa, for today we had a brisk breeze and about two o'clock in the afternoon a tolerable squall which destroyed our mizzen topgallant mast. It did not continue long, fortunately. A few hours previous we had seen hundreds of porpoises at all sorts of gambols. The sea was absolutely alive with them for a short time. Harpoons and guns were brought out to attack them, but I fancy they must have received some secret intelligence of the preparations for warfare, for as soon as the implements were ready they suddenly disappeared and we saw no more of them. They proved correct barometers.

5

Rounding the Cape in a Storm

August 7th – About sunrise this morning we came in sight of the island of Trinidad Martin Vas, which is situated in Latitude 20 degrees 30 seconds Long. 29 degrees. 9 seconds. It is very small, being only about six miles in circumference, but curious high lands. But we were glad that we saw it, as it gave us an opportunity of rating our chronometers, which proved quite correct. Wind not very fair.

August 15th – … Our progress since we crossed the line has been exceedingly slow and tedious, averaging very little more than a degree a day. On Friday afternoon we crossed the tropic of Capricorn and at that time and during the whole of the 14th Saturday we had a brisk and favourable wind which we flattered ourselves would continue with us and take us quickly to the cape, but on rising this morning we found all our bright prospects vanished. It was almost calm and what wind there was, not very fair. It is rather unfortunate because it obliges us to be very careful of the water, and the men in consequence are dissatisfied and say they have not sufficient to allow them to have soup, but we are convinced that it arises from want of management on their part. For since we have had our quantity regularly measured out to us (five pints per day) we find it more than sufficient, although we use it for our ablutions. *[These further restrictions on the use of water were the next step towards serious problems with the crew. For them, soup was a vital part of their meagre diet.]*

August 18th – Catherine came in to me this evening to announce the accouchement of Mrs. Bess, an event which seemed to create a great degree of interest with all on board. She enriched us, to use Mr. Roe's expression, "with eight elegant little pigs".

August 19th – Our situation on the chart today was Lat. 28 deg. 40 sec. Long. 13 deg. 20 sec. The wind at last (after tantalising us for three weeks) really seems now inclined to befriend us. For more than twenty-four hours we have been going from six to eight knots per hour, and there is every appearance of our progress continuing good. But the wind has hitherto proved such a fickle and uncertain friend that it is impossible to place the least reliance upon it.

Many birds called Cape Pigeons have been flying about lately. The Doctor has been very anxious to catch some and for that purpose has had a bait out for several days, but hitherto it has proved unsuccessful.

August 25th – The weather during the last week has been most changeable and unfavourable, alternately calms and contrary gales, the ship rolling and pitching and performing all kinds of antics. On the 23rd and the 24th we experienced a very severe gale although thanks be to our Almighty Protector we rode safely through it without sustaining any injury. The sea washed over the decks too much to allow me to remain there, but I stood a short time at the companion door looking at the awful sublimity of the scene. The sea was literally rolling mountains high, and to use Bishop Heber's words.

"It was no insufficient specimen of those gigantic waves of which I have often heard as prevailing in these latitudes. The deep blue of the sea, the snow white tops of the water, their enormous sweep, the alternate sinking and rising of the ship, which seems like a plaything in a giant's hands, constitute a picture of the most impressive and magnificent character." *[Heber wrote travelogues. He was bishop of Calcutta 1823-26.]* And to add to the scene, whilst I was gazing at it, the heavens were adorned by a rainbow, one of the most perfect in form and colour I ever beheld. I could not help thinking what distress and anxiety my poor mother would have suffered could she but have seen through a glass our situation. The men say it is nothing to what we shall see. For my part, I have no ambition to attain a higher degree of knowledge respecting a storm. I should be perfectly content to remain in my present state of ignorance on the subject. Tom says, in his numerous voyages across the Atlantic, he has never but once seen anything worse. We had however sufficient wind to oblige us to sail under close reefed topsail and reefed mainsail and to render the ship exceedingly wet and uncomfortable, and notwithstanding the greater knowledge and experience of the men I shall not consider my self guilty of exaggeration if upon my return home I tell my friends we encountered a very severe gale off the Cape. We probably should not have felt it so much as we did if the wind had been more favourable. It only just enabled us to lay our course.

Today, at least this evening, it is quite calm, our progress is exceedingly tedious and now I believe our passage must unavoidably be a long one. We have constantly a number of beautiful birds flying around the ship – Cape Pigeons, albatrosses, etc – which have been tempted in vain with most delicate pieces of pork and fat. They have not had prudence enough to resist the bait but the hooks and lines have not been sufficiently strong. This morning a most beautiful and majestic bird was hooked, but by some mismanagement or deficiency in the tackle, it escaped, to the disappointment of all the spectators.

The little pigs have weathered the storm wonderfully; the temperature is becoming exceedingly cold, equal in my opinion, to an English February. On the 24th there was frost and snow.

September 2nd – A total eclipse of the moon took place this evening, which gratified me exceedingly as I never recollect seeing a similar occurrence. The night was rather cloudy but the clouds occasionally dispersed and afforded us an opportunity of observing very distinctly the progress of the shadow. We were forcibly reminded of our friends, thinking how many of those most dear to us might be gazing at the same object that we were precisely at the same moment.

September 5th – This day being in Lat. 38 deg. 15 sec. Long. 20 deg. We may consider ourselves fairly round the Cape. After having been tossing about in its vicinity for fifteen days and although we have not had any very seriously bad weather it has been sufficiently bad to make the ship wet and uncomfortable most of the time and induce all of us to wish we were again in fine weather. We have at present a favourable breeze, which if it will continue with us will soon, we hope, take us out of the way of everything unpleasant. We have now entered the Indian Ocean. Yesterday, September 4th, one of the poor birds was caught, about which the Doctor and Tom have long been so anxious. After satisfying their curiosity by examining its appearance, they tied a ticket around its neck stating our position, etc, and consigned it to its element again.

.... Monday September 13th – A most serious catastrophe had almost befallen us. No less than the loss of our steward – but the fates perceiving to what a miserable condition we should be reduced by such a misfortune, kindly averted the dreadful calamity. His skill as a *cuisenaire* he thinks unequalled. Indeed he has a most exalted idea of his own abilities altogether. Yesterday he begged I would allow him to make a kind of pudding, which according to his account was the finest French dish that could be made. I consented. He told me he must have a piece of new calico to boil it in, which I gave him. But when the pudding made its appearance, it fell far short of our expectations, and very far from his description, it was so insipid that we merely tasted it and sent it away. This morning by way of a joke the Captain told the steward that we had been told he had been so dirty as to boil the pudding in his nightcap. But he took it in earnest, for he said he could not suppose the Captain would tell him a lie, so when we were at dinner he went on deck and got the cloth washed and dried, boasting to the men how he would convince us all of our error. But as soon as he was out of sight, one of the men, to keep up the joke, got his nightcap and rolled it up in the cloth. In the afternoon the Captain, Tom and I were standing together on the quarterdeck. The steward took advantage of the opportunity and came boldly to us to vindicate his wounded reputation

"I have been accused," says he, "of having boiled the pudden in my nightcap. I have brought this to show it is the piece of calico Mrs. Ripley gave me for the purpose, and you may see it has been used." Upon which Tom began to unfold and examine it, when O! Misericord, out fell the luckless nightcap. I wish I had either the pencil of Cruickshank or the pen of Cervantes, to describe the effect upon our poor steward. His countenance changed instantly and he was almost struck mute; it was like an apparition to him. His first act upon returning to his senses was to throw the innocent cause of his distress overboard. He then in great bustle, carried his trunk to the forecastle and declared he would no longer be subject to such indignities. He said he would work as a sailor although when the Captain asked him if he could take his turn at the wheel *[he said]*

"No, Sir, but I can sweep the decks."

A sad degradation from making the finest French dishes – however in the course of the evening he returned to his post, though much broken in spirit, for, he said to me

"The men will now laugh at me so I shall be obliged to carry my head in my bosom."

He threatened dreadful vengeance upon the person who had tricked him, but of course, no one would acknowledge to it. The scene upon deck was so truly ludicrous that Tom scarcely ceased laughing the whole evening.

Monday September 20th – Rose this morning after a perfectly sleepless night, blowing almost a hurricane. According to Mr. Roe's account, the most melancholy sea and melancholy night he ever witnessed. The bosun says he has not experienced such a night for ten years, so that we freshwater sailors, as they call us, might well think it a severe gale … we sustained no damage of any consequence and the storm did not continue many hours, but we felt the effects for some time after the wind had subsided, the vessel rolling most dreadfully. But we consoled ourselves by reflecting that we were proceeding on our way at the rate of two hundred miles per day.

Wednesday September 22nd – According to calculation, if the night proved clear, we were expected to be in sight of St. Paul's Island Lat. 38 deg. 44 sec. Long. 77 deg. 53 sec. South and if the morning, Thursday, proved moderate and fine and we were near it, the gentlemen intended to go on shore. It is particularly famous for fish, which are caught there in astonishing quantities ...

No land seen, and the day proved so thick and hazy that it was impossible to take observations. There was every reason to believe, however, that we were in the vicinity of land as large quantities of seaweed and immense numbers of small birds were seen all morning.

Friday 24th – The Captain found by observation today that it was in consequence of being considerably to the north that we had not seen St Paul's, which he attributed to bad steering, our helmsmen none of them having the character of being great proficients. The beautiful large birds, which first appeared to us in the neighbourhood of the Cape, still continue to accompany us in great numbers and afford constant amusement to Tom and the Doctor, who delight almost daily in proving themselves as good shots at their expense. They are immensely large and very majestic. The gentlemen think with their wings extended they would almost reach across the vessel; they are called albatross of the petrel species. *[The wingspan of the albatross can be up to 11 feet, or 3.5 m – compared with the 28 feet width of the ship.[90] Obviously Tom did not share the belief of some seamen that killing an albatross would bring bad luck to the ship.]* I should like to have seen them on board. We have caught several of the smaller kind, called Cape Pigeons, but the large ones are not so easily enticed. I had nearly forgot to mention that a short time before we reached the longitude of St. Paul's a poor snipe was blown on board. I do not recollect our situation exactly, but it must have been a very considerable distance from home, poor thing, we intended keeping it until we approached St Paul's and then restoring it to land and liberty, but it was so exhausted that a few hours closed its existence

– alas poor snipe!!!

Sunday October 3rd – Our progress has been beyond all our expectations favourable during the last month. The wind, 'the fickle, the inconstant wind', has proved a faithful friend since we passed the Cape, and our forebodings then of a long and tedious passage seem likely to be incorrect. Today at twelve o'clock, we again crossed the Tropic of Capricorn Long. 100 deg. 38 sec. We got the southeast trade delightfully, without any calms or drawbacks of any description. We have an eight and a half knot breeze with every appearance of a continuance and we begin to flatter ourselves that we shall be making Java Head on Saturday next. I shall astonish my friends (indeed I have been very much surprised at it myself) when I send them word that, with the exception of about a fortnight or three weeks when we were near the equator, we have been in cold weather ever since we left England, and the last six weeks have been so cold that I have been obliged to wear both shawl and cloak on deck. Mr. Roe says he never felt it so cold in his life, but he uses the hyperbole as an excuse for a dram. Today the temperature is very perceptibly warmer, but the breeze is so stiff that we probably do not feel it so warm as we otherwise might expect in this latitude. I could dispense with my shawl, however.

October 12th – 'All that's bright must fade, the brightest still the fleetest', so says Tom Moore, and so says Julia Ripley, with too much truth alas in this instance. Our prospects, which were so brilliant last week, have vanished and 'like the baseless fabric of a vision left not a rack behind'. *[Julia is quoting Prospero's speech from Shakespeare's play* The Tempest.*]*

[This was] in consequence of our Captain making *[for]* the Island of Enggano by the direction of Horsburgh without sufficient reference to the wind by which we were favoured,

making a direct run through the Straits of Sunda.[91] *[The Bencoolen's captain appears to have been using the charts of James Horsburgh.]*And having once got out of our way, we find it a more difficult thing to beat back again. We have now been four days in regaining eighty miles and it is impossible to say when we shall arrive at our port although we are only two or three days from it.

Such a circumstance could not have occurred at a more unfortunate time for anticipating such a speedy arrival we had begun to make free with the water, coffee, etc, and are now obliged to reduce our allowance of water to four pints a day, and the men's coffee to a much smaller quantity than they have been accustomed to during the voyage. This has occasioned great discontent among them. In fact almost amounting to mutiny. There are several <u>black sheep</u> amongst them, and the Captain is so exceedingly spiritless and tame that he absolutely dare not speak to them and I much fear we shall have nothing like discipline kept in the ship the whole voyage. We are in hope however that some of the bad ones will take French leave when we get to Batavia.

October 14th – It is very true that we never know the value of anything until we feel the want of it. How I should prize a few of the many quarts of water, which I have wasted in my life. I have never been accustomed before to reflect that scarcely anything, however trifling, can be prepared for eating without water. We are obliged for the present to dispense with bread, soups, and we cannot even afford enough to boil a little rice, for the weather during the last fortnight has become so exceptionally warm that we feel inclined to drink all day.

Java: Feasting Upon Pineapple

Today we had a most delightful shower, which lasted about ten minutes. Tom with his usual expedition arranged a sheet in such a way that he caught four or five gallons of very fine water and I in my small way through my drawing room window, contrived to secure nearly two gallons. The affairs of our ship are so improvidentially managed that the rain is generally over (when we have a shower) before preparations are completed for catching it, so that the men only secured a few buckets full.

Our prospects today are more favourable than they have been for two or three days – we have been enabled to lie more to the East and I trust a short time more will end our difficulties.

October 15th – This evening knowing ourselves to be near the shores of Sumatra, we were all very anxious that land should be discovered. We were very much amused about eleven o'clock to hear the Captain cry out,

"Mr. Ripley, I smell the land!"

I ran upon deck immediately, and certainly did perceive a

very balmy odour, and shortly after there were such strong symptoms of being near shore that we were obliged to tack. We were all upon deck by sunrise again, and it was a great relief to us to be able to ascertain our situation precisely for it is nearly seventy days since we have seen any land and eighty since we fell in with a vessel and we felt unsure as to the state of our chronometer. As the day advanced, the landscape became beautiful. It was fine, bold, high land and the prospect was terminated by a small island, which was completely covered with coconut trees and looked very green and pretty. The water was as smooth as a lake, indeed I could almost have fancied myself upon one of the lovely Swiss lakes, and I sat looking at the picture through the stern ports. For some time we continued within two or three miles of shore and we were in hopes some of the natives would have come off to us and brought us fish, fruit and vegetables, but we were disappointed. Being within sight of land, and consequently able to procure water in case of need, we have all full allowance again, six pints.

Forgot to mention my employment on the afternoon of the 15th, the piratical character of *[some of]* the Malays is well known; we judged it prudent to make preparations for defence in case of attack. Upon examining the ammunition we found that there were no cartridges for the guns. I set to work immediately and with Catherine's assistance we made sufficient for five or six rounds. I could not help thinking how my poor mother would be alarmed if she could see me so engaged. I hope we shall have no occasion to try their efficiency, but it is quite necessary to be prepared. *[The danger from pirates was very real. L. A Mills writes that during the 1830s 'the straits of Malacca swarmed with pirates, Malay, Lanun, and Balanini, and their fleets infested the waters near Malacca, Singapore and Penang. There were pirates in fleets, and in single praus, pirates in big hundred-oared galleys, pirates in small galleys, in rowboats, and solitary pirates in tiny skiffs. The great pirate mart at Galang did a flourishing trade in booty and captives'.*[92]*]*

October 27th – My patience has had such a severe trial for the last twelve days that I really have felt no inclination for continuing my journal or indeed settling myself to any employment; to have been detained a fortnight or more by contrary winds or any unavoidable circumstance would not have vexed me half so much, but to arise from the ignorance or ill judgement of the Captain was exceedingly mortifying. Since the 10th we have been beating about within two days of our port and not able to arrive at it until this morning, when we anchored safely, thanks to our Heavenly Protector, in Batavia roads *[the shipping roads were just outside the port now known as Jakarta]*, amongst five or six of our own country's ships, and one of the number, the *Meredith*. *[So the race had been lost.]* She has been safe in port nearly three weeks which we might very easily have been had we had a more experienced Captain.

The scenery we have sailed through for the last ten days has been beautiful and if we had not been so much out of time I really think we should have enjoyed it very much. This morning for the first time we were boarded by some natives, who came in their canoes to supply us with fruit. I have been literally feasting myself upon pineapple all day. What would our friends in England think of getting large pineapples besides a great quantity of coconuts, plantains, yams, sweet potato, cucumbers, etc, for a Spanish dollar? The natives seem to be … able to make themselves very well understood in English. They are a dark copper colour, they wear scarcely any dress, their hair … is long and glossy, quite black, and I observed several of them had it fastened up by an ornamental comb, but all that we have seen today have had a fancy handkerchief tied about their heads.

Several gentlemen came on board but I could not learn who they were. Captain Fullerton *[of the Meredith]* paid us a visit immediately. *[Perhaps to exalt in his victory, or possibly to collect his winnings. Nevertheless, the rivals remained friends.]* Tom went on shore with him and of course we were not forgotten by the customhouse officers.

I wish I could transport a letter by magic this afternoon to Islington *[in Liverpool]*. What delight it would produce! I hope an early opportunity will occur of sending news to our beloved friends. How must we support our patience for six or eight months longer?

I must not forget to mention that we had today for dinner a very excellent rice pudding made with some of the eggs we brought from Liverpool. Marian will be glad to hear she adopted such an excellent method of preserving them, I certainly can strongly recommend it.

October 28th – We went on shore this morning, and at the landing place found an old acquaintance waiting with his carriage to conduct me to his house in the country, Mr. Doering, whom I recollected perfectly as soon as I saw him, though I had no idea of meeting with anyone I knew in Batavia. *[Edward Doering was a friend and business acquaintance who worked for the Ripleys' agents in Batavia. He was Prussian by birth[93].]* His residence, which is a complete palace, is situated about three miles in the country, a fairyland absolutely. I was enchanted with the short drive; everything was so novel to me. The roads are excellent, the houses have a most rural and picturesque appearance and the trees are beautiful beyond description, all of the most brilliant verdure, etc, of a kind which in England we are accustomed to see nurtured in the greenhouse and with the utmost attention.

October 29th – I was occupied all morning in arranging my affairs with the *blancheseuse [i.e. she arranged to have her linen laundered]*, a work of no trifling magnitude after a voyage of upwards of four months. The men here perform all domestic duties, even the washing, our operator is a Bengali whose style of dress is very different from the natives who generally speaking have little more covering than decency requires. It is at first rather difficult to distinguish the men from the women, except that the former always wears a handkerchief fancifully tied about their heads, and it is considered disrespectful to appear without one. The women have nothing. The house servants are a little more dressed than the people seen about the lanes and streets, they wear a kind of bed gown, and besides their drawers have a little drapery about their thin legs. The dress of the Bengalis consists of a pair of drawers of scarlet calico with white drapery hanging from their shoulders and a white turban something in the Turkish style. The inhabitants of Batavia and the neighbourhood are not considered genuine Javans. They are called Malays ….

Our host, although a bachelor, has no less than twelve *[servants]*, which would in England be thought almost a sufficient establishment for a nobleman. He has three cooks and is by no means a bon vivant, yet the head of the cuisine is so overpowered with work he is daily threatening to leave his service.

In the afternoon we attended the races, a sport which I little expected to see in Batavia. They are conducted quite à l'anglaise. I was exceedingly amused, not exactly with the racing although the ponies are most beautifully spirited creatures but with the tout ensemble, which presented a scene so different from anything I had witnessed before. The crowd was indeed a motley one. It was composed of Chinese, Malays, Javans, Armenians, Dutch, English, etc, etc. Each in their different costumes.

64

A Javanese Man.

...The pine *[pineapple]* is so abundant it is almost looked upon as a weed when seen in a garden. They tell me it grows in fields just like our turnips. Being so plentiful it is in little estimation here, but I give it decidedly the preference to all other fruits which I have tasted. *[In contrast, the pineapple was the height of fashion in England, where it was extremely difficult to grow. At prestigious parties one pineapple might be displayed as a centrepiece on the dining table. Pineapples were so expensive to buy that some hostesses merely hired one. This had to be returned uneaten the next day.]*

The effect to the eye of a tropical desert is very beautiful.

The mangosteen, of which we hear so much, is scarcely in season yet, but Mr. Baxter (a friend of Mr. Doering's) was kind enough to procure some today for the ladies. They are very highly esteemed here. They are only found on Java and the Moluccas. They are very nice and delicate, but I must confess I do not think they equal their reputation. Fish, poultry, and provisions of every kind appear to be abundant and excellent and the country and climate delightful. The atmosphere is so pure and rarefied. Thus with the thermometer upwards of ninety *[degrees Fahrenheit]* I do not find it so insupportable and oppressive as I frequently have done at home. Everything is of course adapted to a warm climate. The houses, which are chiefly one storey, are very lofty and so constructed that you have always a through draught.

October 30th – This evening we attended the race ball, which was held in the grandstand. We thought ourselves fortunate in having so good an opportunity of seeing the *soir* of Batavia and the neighbourhood, though to be candid there is little beauty to boast of, and fashion does not lend her most efficient aid in setting off what little there is. The ladies appear to be at least ten years behind us in modes, or perhaps they are reviving old fashions, and we are ten years behind them. The scene altogether reminded me of a fancy ball. The stewards were dressed in scarlet frock coats. The orchestra ... was composed of natives, and the attendants, some natives, some Bengalis, and some jockeys. The dance is more varied than in England, first a waltz, then a quadrille, then a country dance. We had a very handsome supper, and returned about twelve much gratified with our evening's entertainment.

October 31st – We held quite a levee this morning *[of business acquaintances]*, Mr. and Mrs. Roberts, Mr. and Mrs. Forrester, Mr. Watson[94], etc, etc, were kind enough to pay their respects and in the evening we took a delightful drive.

November 1st – How can I possibly bring myself to think that we have entered upon the gloomy, melancholy month of November? We went to Batavia accompanied by Mrs. Forrester to look at the lions of the Javan capital and found the sun so excessively hot and powerful that we were afraid of being exposed for a moment to its piercing rays. How differently are our dear friends situated at home? Furs are most likely now in demand, and they are no doubt glad of the exhilarating influence of a cheerful, blazing fire. *[Julia's circle of friends in Liverpool were obviously quite privileged. At the opposite end of the social scale were those who did not own a pair of boots, let alone furs!].*

We were disappointed with our morning's employment, for we fancied we should have seen many Chinese and Japan curiosities, but our friends conducted us only to shops of English goods where we saw such trumpery as at home we should not look. At one of the shops there were certainly some splendid specimens of Japan furniture such as I never saw before, but at terrific prices; for instance, nothing less than sixty pounds or seventy pounds … *[At this time the English did not trade directly with Japan, but the Dutch did. This was a rare opportunity for the Ripleys to see Japanese merchandise.]*

November 3rd – We dined with Mr. and Mrs. Roberts today *[to celebrate Julia's birthday]* and I do not ever recollect sitting down to a more splendid entertainment. Our party consisted of upwards of twenty of the principal people of Batavia and we were attended by about as many servants. The table literally groaned beneath the hospitality of our kind friends. Mrs. Roberts is a native born lady; I have seldom seen a more pleasing, more ladylike woman. The parties are conducted here with so much ease and freedom that they are really very agreeable and I think that after the specimens I have seen the residents here would not at all enjoy a stiff and formal English party. We danced in the evening and returned at eleven.

November 5th – We had a splendid entertainment today at the house of Mr. Forrester, a band of music during dinner – a dance in the evening – and everything in fact capable of producing hilarity and pleasure.

7

Wealth Acquired at the Expense of Men's Lives

November 6th – We set out at five this morning upon an excursion to Buitenzorg, the residence of the governor, about thirty-five miles from Batavia. *[The elegant country house 'Buitenzorg' was built by the Dutch Governor General, Van Imhoff. It became the residence of subsequent governors of Java, including Sir Stamford Raffles during the brief period of British domination of the island at the end of the Napoleonic Wars. The name Buitenzorg means 'without a care'. The area is now known as Bogor.]*

We formed a party of eight, having the addition to our own circle of two of Mr. Doering's intimate friends, Mr. Watson and Mr. Baxter. We arrived to breakfast about half past nine, after a most charming ride, every step of the horses presenting something new to me, which I had never seen before. The scenery during the latter half of the ride was exceedingly rich and beautiful. A fine chain of hills almost covered to the summit with verdure and foliage formed the background and all around us were innumerable objects of interest, especially the sawaks or rice grounds.

Rice forms the principal article of subsistence to the natives, consequently their chief attention is directed towards its cultivation, which appears much more complicated and troublesome than I had any idea of and am surprised how it can be produced at so cheap a rate as it is. We saw the land chiefly in a state of irrigation, which in fact is the most important part of the process, for where they cannot convey the water the land is of little or no value. The cultivators have many enemies to contend with, such as rats, birds, etc, etc. To frighten away the latter they have a very amusing contrivance, they erect very picturesque looking sheds upon poles of a considerable height, from which are attached ropes from one to another, with scarecrows fastened to them. There are people continually in the sheds after the grain is up, and as soon as they perceive a flight of birds they pull the ropes and frighten them away. The ploughs, etc, are all drawn by buffalos and the people take so much care of, and are so fond of these animals that our informants say it grieves them much more to lose a buffalo than a brother. Their carts are most picturesque; I should very much like a model of one of them. They look just like straw-built cottages. They are all covered, no doubt, to protect the people from the sun.

We passed several fields of indigo and a few of sugar and pineapples, almost every tree too was new to me, but the banana, the coconut, and the bamboo are more decidedly *[East]* Indian-looking than any of the rest, and to a stranger, give a very striking effect to the landscape.

Amongst the mountains we saw one that was continually burning, it has never, I believe, produced an eruption. We were told before going to Buitenzorg that it invariably rains there in the afternoon, so that when it commenced, although it confined us to the house for the rest of the day, we were not disappointed. The gentlemen amused themselves with billiards, and we talked and looked on. We did not forget to drink my dear father's health. I sincerely hope that he is in tolerable health and that he will be spared to enjoy many happy years. *[Julia was anxious about her father because she knew that he was not in the best of health].*

November 7th – Rose again this morning about five o'clock that we might take advantage of the morning for seeing the lions of Buitenzorg. We rambled for two or three hours through the park attached to the palace of the Governor.[95] It is a most delightful place and nature has done as much for it both as regards climate, soil, and situation, that the chief art that is requisite is to keep under the luxuriousness of the weeds.

In a very romantic and beautiful part of the grounds is a monument erected to the memory of the first Lady Raffles, who died in Batavia, but it does not deserve much eulogism, it is rather paltry. It is only built of brick and is plastered over. *[Sir Thomas Stamford Raffles was a governor of Batavia for a short while, during the time that Java was in British hands. Lady Raffles and several of her children died of disease there, despite its reputation for being a healthy place. By the time of the Ripleys' visit, Java was back under Dutch administration.]*

The Governors certainly show most excellent taste in residing at this delightful place rather than Batavia, and besides the beauty of it, it has such a decided advantage in point of salubrity. Being so near to the mountains, it is considerably cooler, and in fact is so healthy that the hotel is much resorted to by invalids. We returned to breakfast at nine o'clock and gave most convincing proofs that our walk had not been injurious to our appetites. After breakfast, carriages were ordered and we took a most delightful drive stopping on the way to see some remains of very great antiquity. One of them is a stone with an inscription, which as yet antiquaries have not been able to decipher.[96]

Upon our return, we found some dancing girls awaiting our arrival. All over Java they are held in great estimation. They performed to their national music. …their chief skill is displayed in the use of their fingers and fans.

Some of the gents (and amongst the number Tom) went through the operation of *champooing [a kind of therapeutic massage]*, a ceremony I was not aware was going to be performed, or I would most certainly have been present at the exhibition. Not being a spectator I am not competent to describe the process, but I believe it consists chiefly in cracking all the joints. It is attended with a little pain, and is said to be administered as a substitute for exercise …. a <u>dose of champooing</u> is considered equal to five or six miles of walking. Tom, I understand, was a minute or two before he felt quite convinced that the man had not actually put his neck out.

November 8th – Arrived back in Batavia at half past eight to breakfast, having been only three hours and a half in performing thirty-six miles, most astonishingly quick travelling for a tropical country. Indeed we should not have posted more swiftly in England than nearly eleven miles an hour. We all returned exceedingly delighted with our excursion although for such rapid travelling of course we had to pay pretty handsomely. Tom's share of the expense for a two days trip was thirteen pounds.

I begin to suffer dreadfully in consequence of the mosquito bites. I have unfortunately been impatient and rubbed one of my legs until the skin is broken and today it is so dreadfully swelled and painful that I fear I shall find it troublesome. The swelling is probably much increased by the exercise, which I took yesterday after being so long unaccustomed to walking.

November 16th – We have led a remarkably quiet life since our return from Buitenzorg … Sunday the 14th I attended church for the first time for five months. Afterwards we called upon Mr. and Mrs. Roberts and partook of a very sumptuous Tiffin.

November 21st - We have paid several farewell visits this week. It is the custom here to make calls in the evening, as in the morning the ladies all indulge in a siesta. The houses are all closed and they go regularly to bed.

It is a novel sight to an Englishman to see the lights by which the carriages are illuminated by night. The footmen carry large sticks of lighted bamboo, which make a tremendous blaze. If our nightly equipage was seen in London, good folks would think we had just arrived from the infernal regions.

November 22nd – Tom has just brought me the unpleasant intelligence that one of our best men is dead. This is the second, one having been carried off a few days previous. It really shocks me very much to hear of such mortality amongst them and almost dread and dislike the wealth acquired at the expense of so many men's lives. The Doctor is also at the hotel, either sick or dreadfully frightened, but we suspect the latter *[it was the former]*. For ourselves (being in the country) we have not felt the slightest indisposition, but undoubtedly the town and roads have not acquired their unhealthy character undeservedly. God's ways are inscrutable, he gives and takes life at pleasure, but I humbly pray him that it may be his good will that he may spare <u>us all</u> that remain, and to have mercy upon those he has removed.

…. We have Mr Baxter as a passenger to Singapore. He is an intimate friend of Mr Doering's, a military man, very gentlemanly and very agreeable.

We spent the afternoon at Mrs. Roberts and in the evening

took a delightful drive to hear the music of a military band, which plays three times a week and is attended by all the rank and fashion of Batavia.

Singapore: Mutiny on the *Bencoolen*

December 16th – Nearly a month has elapsed since I have had industry and courage enough to continue my journal …. We quitted Batavia on the 24th of November and I must say with a little regret, having met with many kind and hospitable friends, several of whom accompanied us on board the vessel and spent the afternoon with us. They partook very freely of our champagne, and when they bid us adieu, were not a little merry.

By daylight on the 25th *[of November]* we weighed anchor and performed our passage to Singapore in a much shorter space of time than we ever anticipated. Our Batavian friends having comforted us by telling us we should do very well if we got to Singapore in a month, instead of which we arrived in twelve days. I must say we were indebted in a great measure to Tom for our despatch, for he kept a constant watch upon the currents, charts, etc and the navigation through the straits is so intricate that being strangers by nothing but extreme care and vigilance could we have made so good a voyage. The scenery is particularly beautiful, the waters seem to be studded all over with islands covered with verdure of the brightest hue, and frequently I have looked around with astonishment, wondering where we could possibly find a passage for the ship to go through. The weather was not agreeable, alternately squalls and calms, and during the squalls I could not help feeling anxious and nervous, as they were attended by heavy rain that it was impossible to see a hundred *[yards]* around us. However, we got safely through them, and anchored at Singapore on the 6th of December, too late in the evening to go on shore.

December 7th – immediately after breakfast Tom, Mr. Baxter *[a passenger from Batavia]*, and the Captain went on shore and returned soon after accompanied by Mr. Diggles to fetch me. *[Robert Diggles worked for Syme and Co., the Ripleys' agents in Singapore.97]*

When I arrived on shore I was happy to find Mrs. Strachan prepared for my reception. The house she occupies is delightfully situated about a mile and a half from the town of Singapore. *[The house was known as Duxton and was near Spottiswode Park. It belonged to Syme and Co., and in 1836 the estate of Duxton was 'sixteen acres planted with spice and other fruit trees, with a commodious dwelling house'.98]*

December 16th – We have been here now ten days. Our friends are very attentive and kind to us, but I must confess I should prefer Batavia as a residence to Singapore. There is of course much more English society here, because this is an English colony, but there is a great deal of ceremony and etiquette observed, so much so that if a No. 1 (for there are two numbers) should be seen speaking to a No. 2 … No. 1 must directly be degraded from his elevated station. Besides this, there is a spirit of littleness and interference into each other's concerns99, which is generally found in provincial places, and the place is so limited as to the possibility of escaping from the gossip and scandal, though it is an astonishing colony. *[In June 1830 Singapore lost its 'presidency' status, and was reduced to a 'residency' for a brief time; this may have contributed to the atmosphere of bitterness and dissatisfaction noticed by Julia Ripley].* Its rise has been exceedingly rapid; it is little more than ten years since Sir Stamford Raffles fixed upon the situation as one likely to be advantageous and safe. It was then nothing, a fishing hamlet, and now it is a town of some commercial importance. The island, which was almost unimpenetrable jungle, is now in part cleared and cultivated, and excellent roads are made to the extent of three or four miles round the town. *[How much more astonished the Ripleys would be if they could see Singapore today!]*

Provisions of every kind are scarce and dear, especially animal food, which is considered a great treat. Being chiefly English residents, the domestic arrangements and comforts are more congenial at least, if not better than in Batavia …

A Palanquin

We drive out every evening between dinner and ten, but as the roads extend so short a distance, we are obliged to take the same *[route]* every day. There is no variety; there is not the same picturesque beautiful country that we were accustomed to in Java. The carriages here are very inferior and very ugly. They are called palanquins, drawn by one horse, and look just like hearses, except that they are not decked out with feathers.

Upon the whole I should certainly not like Singapore as a place of residence and I fear we shall be detained much longer than we anticipated upon our arrival, for we are most distressingly situated. A mutiny (a catastrophe which I have long predicted) has broken out in the *Bencoolen*. In consequence, there is almost an entire cessation of work, and what is the most unpleasant part of it is that those upon whom we placed the greatest reliance have proved the worst, namely, the second mate Mr. Carr, and the carpenter. By some means or other they have got access to drink and in the words of the boatswain they have been mad for several days. Their conduct became so alarming at last that policemen were obliged to be sent on board to convey them to prison, where they are to remain until we sail, and if possible, until we return from Manila. I almost dread putting ourselves into their power again for they are now in such a state that I should not be surprised at anything they would do. But surely there is an almighty and protecting arm above that will preserve us from all evil machinations. He has brought us thus far in safety, and I humbly trust will grant us a happy meeting again with our beloved friends and relatives, if it be His blessed will and pleasure.

Mr. Strachan arrived unexpectedly to dinner today, by a Portuguese vessel; Mrs S. of course quite overjoyed to see him after five months absence.

Tom dined one day with the Resident *[of Singapore]*, Mr.

Ibbetson[100], and another with the officers at the mess *[the 11th Madras Native Infantry[101]]*, played at whist each time, and was particularly unfortunate. Dollar points is the usual stake here and in the two nights he lost eighty dollars without betting.

January 30th – Alas poor journal! It is now more than a month since I have noted down one single occurrence and how I shall be able to recall to memory the events of five weeks I cannot possibly tell …

Mrs Strachan, *[was]* unfortunately confined to her rooms almost the whole time we were in her house *[due to illness]*. I should have found it very dull had it not been for her friend Mrs. Stott, the wife of the commanding officer[102], who spent most of her time with me. I found her very kind-hearted and agreeable, which is not the character of the good folks in Singapore generally, they are with few exceptions, proud and selfish. Tom dined out occasionally and several times at the mess with the officers, whom he found much more agreeable than the rest of society.

Christmas Day, I think I shall never forget it. I can scarcely persuade myself that Christmas has arrived. I devoted the greater part of the day to corresponding with my friends and how could I fancy it Christmas, sitting as I was in an open veranda, almost overpowered by the intensity of the heat? The trees and shrubs all around me in luxurious leaf and bloom – no frost and snow, no cheerful blazing fire, and no beloved friends to give the annual salute and compliments of the season. The only indication of the day was some English mince pies, perhaps the very first that ever were seen at Singapore, they were excellent. Under the circumstances I could not feel cheerful, and I fear our absence would throw a damp upon the usual merry party in Islington. If it please God that we return in safety to our beloved home and find all well there, we must hope to make amends next year for the deprivation of this, by a double portion of happiness and mirth.

Mrs. Stott took me kindly one evening to drink tea in the Chinese style at a pagoda. We were received I may say enthusiastically by the priest who seemed delighted at the honour we had done him by visiting him. A Chinese tea drinking is quite a burlesque, the equipage is just upon the scale of a dolls, and when I show the little tea pots in England, which they use upon these occasions, I am sure the good people will think I am joking. The ingredient, however, is of the finest quality, and used (in proportion to the size of the teapot) in profusion. No sugar is put into the tea, but a piece of sugar candy kept in the mouth while drinking it. We of course could not understand a word the good man said to us, nor was our language intelligible to him. However, we appeared delighted with his little establishment, and after we had taken as much tea as was convenient, to give us a more convincing proof of his hospitality he produced a large square bottle of strong arrack, and pouring out a tumbler full, presented it to me. I was just in the act of tasting it when our gentlemen, who were to follow us, made their appearance and were not a little amused at the scene, which they witnessed.

The priest proved himself decidedly a man of taste. He evidently preferred the society of ladies, and though he certainly treated the gentlemen with tea, he neither made it so good for them nor gave it to them apparently with such good will. The gents walked home, and Mrs. Stott and I returned in her palanquin, a description of carriage, which is universal in Singapore, and as ugly as it is general. It reminds me of a bathing machine… It is drawn by one horse and a coachman or Syze, as he is called, runs always at the horse's head. Upon speaking of their extreme unsightliness, the people argue that they are very useful, but I cannot understand why a little elegance might not be united with utility.

Our crew continued in a complete state of insubordination, and about a week before we left a man of war arrived (the *Crocodile*) and all the men that were discontented were discharged and sent on board the frigate. It was commanded by the honourable Captain Montagu – he dined at Mr. Stachan's – a very gentlemanly man[103].

[The 'very gentlemanly' Captain Montagu was the grandson of an admiral. Since 1820 he had been actively employed in the suppression of smuggling, until 1828 when he took command of the HMS Crocodile, a 28-gun sloop. She was a wooden sailing vessel of 500 tons. British naval vessels cruising in eastern waters frequently became short of men as members of the crew died of tropical and other diseases. Since British naval vessels had to be manned by British crews, captains would resort to sending a press gang onto any British merchant vessel in the vicinity[104] However, it appears that Thomas Ripley, ever the opportunist, actually offered the mutinous part of his crew to the Navy - the action of a very ruthless man.]

9

Dangerous Seas Near the Spice Islands

This defection of our crew obliged us to get a crew of Bengalis and we have found ourselves much more comfortable with them. We have a famous ship full of people – thirty Bengalis, fourteen of our old crew, Mr. and Mrs. Strachan and two domestics, Mr. Clegg, Mr. Merryweather and servants, and our noble selves, altogether nearly sixty people, so that in case of need we could make a little resistance against pirates. *[This time the* Bencoolen *was carrying a valuable cargo including gold dust.*[105]*]*

We embarked on the 8th of January and had a large and merry party to dinner, consisting of Captain and Mrs. Stott, all the officers, and some other gentlemen with whom we had been most intimate in Singapore. The party being too large for the cabin, a table was erected upon the quarterdeck. Mrs. Strachan, who continued a great invalid, did not come on board until evening. All thought very highly of our accommodations. Most of the gentlemen remained until a late hour, and left us having apparently enjoyed themselves very much.

A little after daylight on the 9th, Mr Diggles and two or

three of his friends came on board to say goodbye again. They kindly brought us some bottles of milk for breakfast. About seven a nice fresh breeze sprang up, we immediately weighed anchor, and about eight once more began to ride merrily through the water. The monsoon being against us, we were obliged to proceed to Manila by what is called the Eastern Passage, as it is next to impossibility to beat up the China Sea. The winds and more particularly the currents are so exceedingly strong. *[It was not until the tall clipper ship was designed that vessels were able to beat up the China Sea, and save a great deal of travelling time.]*

This is the 22nd of January, and we have made most astonishing progress. We have just been fourteen days at sea, and we have performed considerably more than half our distance and what is still better, we have got over the greatest difficulties. We are now in the Gillola Passage. … It is a very interesting voyage, a great part of the way being amongst the Spice Islands. But I do not think the scenery will compare with that in the Drayon Straits near to Singapore. Nor upon the whole is it such tedious and intricate navigation as between Batavia and Singapore.

On the 15th, however, we were all put in mortal terror, and undoubtedly were in a considerable degree of danger. We had just arrived at the most difficult and dangerous part of our passage, the south entrance to the Straits of Macassar, where the sea is very much choked up by shoals and coral reefs … at the Southern point of the Celebes is very much dreaded shoal called the Brill. In order to avoid this, we got into the very midst of the Macassar Straits. In fact, for two or three hours, we neither knew exactly where we were, nor what to do. All we were certain of was that in one instance about five minutes would have brought us upon an awful reef. It makes me shudder when I think upon it, although at the time I believe I was less alarmed than most of the party. The gentlemen wore dreadfully long faces, though if we had been so unfortunate as to strike, possibly no lives would have been lost. The morning was clear and beautiful and the sea was quite smooth. We were all much provoked at the indifference of the Captain. It did not seem to give him the least concern for having brought us into such a critical situation. He said he never saw people so alarmed in all his life, for he always took these things coolly. In the midst of our dilemma, most providentially the wind changed and carried us quite clear of all dangers, and we were not even aware when we passed the Brill, to avoid which we had been placed in such peril.

During the whole of the night … our progress was perfectly surprising. The night being dark, and not having a long run before coming upon more land we dare not go at full speed, but do what they would, they could not keep our gallant ship back. She had merely her foresail set and her topsails on the cap and independently of this they turned her yards in all positions to escape the wind and withal she went in twelve hours 130 miles. It is almost incredible but it is true – of course there must have been a tremendous current in our favour.

January 24th – This morning we heard the unexpected and unusual exclamation of "a ship in sight!" We hailed her. She was an American from Philadelphia bound to China. Tom wrote a few hasty lines to Henry and took them on board himself. He returned with a large budget of newspapers, which gave us full particulars of the disturbances in France, etc. *[She is referring to the fall of the Bourbon monarchy in the July Revolution of 1830]*.

January 26th - An interesting and amusing incident occurred today. We were approaching the Asia Isles, which are situated about Lat. 1 deg. North and about 131 deg. Long. The Captain was anxious to beat to windward of them, but as we required to go much further to the eastward, Tom advised him to go at once to the leeward, which he did, and immediately upon turning round the corner we saw a boat endeavouring to gain the ship. The wind and the current were too strong to allow of the boat reaching us unless we laid to for her. Some of the party were for it, some against it, urging that there could be no inducement or recompense for the delay, but it appeared such a singular thing, to see a boat coming from islands that seemed to be uninhabited that it was at length agreed to lay to and learn the news. Some were already smacking their lips at the very idea of a fine mess of turtle – and others anticipating a treat of some delicious fruit. But all our airy castles quickly vanished – the contents of the boat were of a very different nature. It was a barque of the rudest and most singular construction. The centre was a canoe, very long and narrow. I should think only one man could sit in the width, and at each side, lying upon the water, were a kind of wings composed of pieces of bamboo fastened together in a sort of trellis work *[outriggers]* to prevent the little vessel from upsetting. It had a sail and the men in it also used paddles. As it approached there was a general cry,

"There are Europeans in it!" - And it really was the case.

There were two Englishmen who described themselves as perishing. They belonged to a whaling vessel that had been cruising amongst the eastern islands. They had gone a party of seven to the Asia Isles to fetch turtles; five had returned to the ship with a boat load intending to return for their companions, but the evening became so thick and stormy that they could not leave the ship again and these poor fellows had been twenty-five days in this wretched situation.

The islands, as we conjectured, were not inhabited, and during the time they had remained upon them they had had nothing to subsist upon but turtle. They had fortunately discovered some fresh water, but their reservoir was almost dry. There was only about an inch remaining, and if they dug deeper it became quite salt. There were no trees or anything to shelter them and though they were not annoyed by mosquitoes, they had enemies of quite as malignant a nature – they were much wounded by the bites of the sandflies. Canoes had arrived frequently from New Guinea and the adjacent islands, numerously manned and they had been obliged to drag wood and work just like slaves for them. I am only surprised they did not carry them away as slaves.

There were three or four *[Papuan]* men there. When *[the Europeans]* saw our vessel … *[they]* made them such large promises if they would take them to the ship that they were at last induced to comply with their request. We of course could not refuse to take them on board, and the 'captain' of the boat also came to receive his reward. He was quite black and had very little more upon him that what nature had blessed him with. When deciding what should be given to him, Tom thought that the most comely present would be a pair of trousers. However, we gave him what we thought would please him better – some old silk handkerchiefs, several yards of grey calico, six or eight pocketknives, and two bottles of rum. He looked very curiously during the presentation, that we could not determine whether he was pleased or dissatisfied. *[The Papuans may well have thought that the Europeans were overdressed, especially Julia. At this time huge sleeves stuffed with feather pillows were the fashion for women]*.

We did not detain them long as we were anxious to proceed on our voyage so we despatched our new black friends and made sail as quickly as possible, all feeling a satisfaction in having waited for the boat, being the means, probably, of saving two fellow creatures from much distress and misery.

Upon the whole we did not think their tale very straightforward, it seemed very strange that they alone, of a whole ship's crew, should have been left behind and especially a cruising vessel. We were inclined to believe them deserters, still their tale might be true - at any rate they must have been sufficiently punished. After getting shaved, washed and dressed, they looked stout able men and they may prove very useful to us, as we shall want Europeans for our homeward passage. One of them is a carpenter, and a very intelligent man.

I have almost forgot to mention the unfortunate death of our poor Doctor – he only survived our departure from Batavia a very short time. Whilst at Singapore we received a letter from Mr. Doering informing us that he died on the evening of the day we left, November the 24th. We both regret his death very much and are sorry we should have been the cause of his leaving his friends and country to be buried amongst strangers. How I pity his poor wife, what distress she will experience when she receives the melancholy intelligence.

From the 24th [of January] until the 4th of 5th of February we experienced nothing but calm and light baffling winds, which tried our patience exceedingly. About the 5th however, we got a regular trade wind, which carried us on delightfully. On the 13th, Sunday, we went round the north of Luconia. We had a most beautiful day and breeze and were not visited by any of the dreadful gales which we had been told almost invariably prevail there. The scenery is very fine but I scarcely ever saw any equal to that immediately before entering the Bay of Manila. We spent nearly the whole of the 7th upon deck, quite in a state of enchantment. In the morning we had a beating wind, the land was of such a bold high character that we sometimes approached it almost within a stone's throw. Occasionally a picturesque looking rock grazing its bold front out of the clear blue water bid us beware.

In the afternoon the wind became quite favourable for running into the bay. About seven in the evening a large ship was seen coming out of the bay, we hailed her and found she was bound to Cadiz. Tom immediately wrote a few lines to Henry, thinking it an excellent opportunity of sending word we were all well. He and Mr. Strachan to learn the Manila news. Our Captain being a little timid dare not venture to run on to Manila in the night, so about eleven or twelve we came to anchor within six or seven miles of our destination.

Friday the 18th February. The morning was most provokingly calm – our anchor was twice taken up under the hopes of having a little breeze, but twice we were disappointed, the third attempt, however, was not in vain, a nice little wind sprung up and about one o'clock we anchored in Manila Bay. A health boat comes always to a ship as soon as she anchors, but we arrived at a most unfortunate time; it was just the hour of siesta, and instead of the doctor and customs house officers coming to see that all was right a boat was sent to remain beside us until afternoon to see that nobody nor anything left the ship. This was very tantalising and obliged Mrs. Strachan and me to give up the idea of going on shore that day to our great disappointment. At four in the afternoon the visit arrived, and to our great astonishment the letter bag was opened and the direction of every letter (amounting I should think to considerably more than a hundred) copied. This, Mr Strachan said, was an entirely new regulation arising in consequence of the intelligence that had been received respecting all the disturbances in France and Holland, and so particular were they that they required all letters to be opened at the police and sometimes read. Two customhouse officers always remain on board. In the evening

Mr. Ker came to pay his respects to us and all our gentlemen accompanied him on shore to make arrangements for us in the following morning. *[Mr. Ker, then aged thirty, also worked for the house of agency, Strachan, Murray & Co., at Manila].*[106]

10

The Philippines: Spanish Dancers and Grass Canoes

According to our time, *[it is]* Saturday the 19th *[of February]*, but Manila time Friday the 18th. We went on shore to breakfast, which we enjoyed very much. When we are in Rome we must do as they do in Rome, so we have been obliged to change our day from Saturday to Friday. *[The Philippines had a difference in time of one day until December 1844.*[107]*]*

Sunday the 20th – We had a complete levee of visitors today, the whole morning being devoted to the ceremony of being introduced to the Spanish and English gentlemen of Mr. Strachan's acquaintance. *[James Strachan was a partner in the company named Strachan, Murray and Co., which was Thomas Ripley's house of agency in Manila. Strachan and his wife had sailed with the Ripleys to Manila, together with another passenger Mr. Merryweather, where they all intended to live in the company house.*[108]*]*

In the evening we drove upon the Calsad or public drive.

I was astonished at the number of carriages. The scene really reminded me of Hyde Park in miniature, only that the carriages were not upon the same scale or splendour as in our great capital …and the ladies … never wear bonnets. …The style in which they dress their hair is very close and small and a huge comb behind which stands up just like a tower about half a yard high without exaggeration.

The climate appears to me to be delightful. It is almost cold in the evenings and the air is dry and light, but we are told that in another fortnight we shall suffer much from the heat, about this time the thermometer ranges from eighty degrees to eighty-six or eighty-seven *[Fahrenheit]*. I have not been so little annoyed by the mosquitoes since I arrived in India, *[in the 1830s the word 'India' was applied to the East Indies as well as to the subcontinent of India]* nor have I met with any other nuisance in the way of insects. The house that we are in is admirably adapted to the climate. It is situated upon the banks of the river and is built with a corridor all around the rooms, which keeps them very cool. It is the plan upon which all the houses are constructed, also the windows being composed of mother of pearl shells, which are well calculated for keeping out the sun.

The establishments in my opinion are much better conducted than either in Singapore or Batavia …. We are more reminded of Europe here than either of the other places. Here too the women seem to be useful members of society. Upon the whole, the first impressions of Manila are very favourable.

Tuesday and Wednesday the 22nd and 23rd were devoted to returning visits; the evenings I mean, and never did I pay visits that amused me more than some of them. The first was upon the wife of the collector of customs. The rooms which he occupies are in the custom house and really very handsome, but his wife and family … certainly prefer and exercise ease before elegance … most of them without stays, and in cotton dresses. We have not yet seen the younger part of females smoking cigars, though we understand it is usual, but old ladies are quite privileged.

Our second call was upon the lady of the intendente (the second man of consequence in the island). She is a lady of elegant manners and the establishment altogether that of a gentleman. Both Mrs Strachan and I, however, found this rather an awful affair, not knowing a single word of the language, and almost as soon as we arrived we were <u>trotted out</u> to play the piano and show off our accomplishments. There were a number of people present, for all visits are made in the evening except Sundays and feast days.

Thursday the 24th – After taking a beautiful drive in the country we went to a ball given by a Spanish lady whose name I do not know. Here again we were highly amused to see the difference of manners and customs from our own. They are most affectionate people, there is such a kissing goes on amongst intimate friends, and we have had to go through the ceremony by those who wish to be very kind to us. Waltzing was altogether the order of the evening. I, not being at all accustomed to that style of dance, did not like to attempt it before strangers who waltz so well. We were so much pressed to dance however that it appeared rude to persist in refusing. So a quadrille was formed for us, but with great difficulty. This was a greater exhibition than bungling through a waltz, for the eyes and attention of the whole party were intently fixed upon 'las inglesas'. So that afterwards we preferred joining the waltz, and of course, according to Spanish politeness, we were complimented upon our first attempt. The heat was intolerable, and although I was exceedingly amused, I was glad when the hour of departure arrived that we might breathe the fresh air.

A ball gown of the 1830s.

The morning I had completely devoted to writing to England and it is no sinecure to be clerk when a ship is going to sail for home and this opportunity via Anjer. Tom's letters were particularly long and explanatory in consequence of the change he has made in his plans. Where we shall go before we return or when that happy event is likely to take place it is quite impossible to say. *[Julia was being secretive because she dared not reveal the plan to smuggle goods into China through the notorious island of Lintin.]* At any rate our absence must be considerably extended for we are going again to Singapore and Batavia, from thence to China, back to Manila and afterwards I know not where. I begin to think we shall not reach home in time to join the Christmas party at Islington. *[It may be that Tom had hoped to get a cargo of rice*

93

to take to China, but the rice was scarce in the Philippines due to a plague of locusts that year. This would explain the need to return to Batavia before going on to China. Rice was grown for export in Java.]

March 6th … We drive every evening and I am delighted with the picturesque beauty of the country, last night instead of our drive we sailed up the river in a banco for half an hour and were much pleased with the change. *[The River Pasig]* It is a very pretty river and of a tolerable width. We continue still to receive and pay visits in the evening, but as the novelty wears off some of them become rather tedious.

March 18th – A scene of considerable novelty took place today, a race between the *Bencoolen's* jollyboat and one of the canoes, a kind of barque, which they call a grass boat *[because it was used for transporting grass]*, one of the lightest description that can possibly be made, usually moved by paddles by one man, but on this occasion two. The only comparison that occurred to me upon seeing the rivals side by side was that of a high metalled racer and a carriage horse. But alas, when put to the test, the poor boat dwindled in point of speed to the pace of a carthorse comparatively speaking; she was completely distanced by the canoe. It was a most animated scene; such an exhibition I suppose never took place before in Manila – the river was crowded with bancas, and every place where the race could be seen was covered with people, all, with very few exceptions, in favour of the canoe. Tom, as usual, chief paymaster. Most of the gentlemen who assembled to witness the race dined with us and in the evening we had a native band and a number of dancing girls …. They use the castanets in all their dances, which makes them very spirited. An opportunity, a very favourable one, afforded for Valparaiso, which I wrote to our friend Mrs White.

Friday the 19th – About four o'clock in the afternoon we embarked for Singapore. I had been a little unwell for three or four days and the doctor did not give his consent to my departure very freely. Mr Strachan and Mr Ker accompanied us on board and remained until nearly nine, I felt much less fatigued by the exertion than I anticipated. I left Mrs Strachan with much regret, she is an exceedingly amiable young woman, I flatter myself she will feel my absence. She will occupy herself very industriously in acquiring the Spanish language and I shall not be in the way to divert her attention from it.

At eleven or perhaps later, we heard the captain's cry,

"All hands to the anchor!"

And then the

"Heave hoy" of the men – we began almost to fear the ship was upon the bar, for after they had been labouring for an hour and a half and she should have been moving for some time, the man at the helm cried out

"She's stock still, sir."

Upon sounding however, there was plenty of water, and with a little assistance from the boat, and a nice little breeze springing up, we got off delightfully, and in the morning we were rejoiced to find how well we had proceeded during the night. I did not feel sufficiently strong to rise until late in the day so that I lost all the beautiful scenery of the entrance to the bay.

26th – About one in the morning Tom was aroused by the captain to go and look at Pulo Sapata, an island situated in Lat. 10 deg. 1 sec. Long. 109 deg. 2 sec. It is high land and it is a kind of signpost coming down the China Sea. Captains always think it advisable to make it. Tom however was very dubious and thought the captain had mistaken some other island for it, for during that day our progress had been almost incredible. But upon taking observations the next day it appeared that we had a current in our favour almost like a sluice. In two days it had drifted us nearly one hundred miles further than we thought we had been.

29th – After a delightful passage of only ten days we anchored in Singapore roads. Tom went on shore intending to have procured accommodations at the hotel for us as our stay was likely to be so short, thinking also that as Mr Diggles' was now completely a bachelor's establishment it might be inconvenient for him to entertain a lady. But he returned immediately with Mr D who had very kindly prepared for us to be his guests and was so pressing that we could scarcely refuse to accept his invitation.

We were sorry to find that all our old military friends had taken their departure for their station at Madras. They had left only a few days before our arrival.

We remained ten days in Singapore during which period I was quite alone in the mornings so that I had plenty of time to write to my friends at home and I had excellent opportunities, for two vessels sailed for London whilst we were on shore.

On the 8th of April we dined at Mr Burn's the clergyman, a very pleasant day. *[The Rev. Robert Burn, B. A. was the government chaplain in Singapore.]*

On the evening of the 9th we embarked for Batavia – Mr Diggles and Mr Whitehead accompanied us on board – the former remained all night. At six o'clock in the morning of the 10th we were aroused by the cry

"Up the anchor!"

Before taking our final leave of Singapore we gave them a salute of nine guns in very good style, which was returned from the fort - also with nine. *[Due to the dangers of eastern voyages, vessels like the* Bencoolen *were pierced for 18 or 20 guns.]* After which we fired three guns just to say "Adieu and thank you". Mr

Diggles bid us goodbye and off we set, but we had a very light wind and made but poor progress until the evening when a breeze sprang up which carried us safely through the Dryon Straits.

11

Indonesia: a Chinese Wedding

April 12th – About six o'clock in the evening we overtook the *Southworth* which left Singapore the day before we did having a strong wind to start with, but we had an advantage over her in being so much lighter and *[in]* better sailing condition. Captain Coombs came on board and spent the evening with us. Tom sent another letter by him to Henry. We were this evening almost at the entrance of the Banka Straits. *[The* Southworth, *350 tons, was a vessel used for the transportation of convicts to Australia. She was returning to Sheerness under Captain Coombs, to pick up another consignment of prisoners.*[109]]*

April 17th – After experiencing calms, light winds, and strong currents all week, we anchored in Batavia roads *[off Jakarta]* this evening about nine o'clock, and considering the weather, flattered ourselves we made a very tolerable passage being only seven days from Singapore.

April 18th – I accompanied Tom on shore this morning. We found Mr. Doering at the door of his godowns *[business premises]* and of course rather surprised him by our appearance at that early hour. He had not heard of the arrival of the *Bencoolen* although he had been in daily expectation of her coming in. I had to remain in town a few hours whilst he sent for the carriage, but my time was most delightfully occupied in perusing despatches from dear "dolce domum" *[sweet home]*. Thank God my beloved relatives were all alive and my dear parents as well as I expected. I sincerely hope and trust the next letters, if I receive any more, may be as favourable. Notwithstanding the size of the budget I felt a little disappointed that I had no later intelligence than the end of August, as several vessels had arrived bringing letters of a much more recent date.

About two o'clock in the afternoon the carriage arrived. I proceeded to the country and was introduced to Mrs. Doering. I had seen her as Miss Jutting upon our last visit here, but was not much acquainted with her. I had not been long in the house, however, before I perceived the magical effect of a lady's hand. Everything appeared so much more comfortable and neat than in our former visit. *[Nineteen-year-old Jeanne Jutting was from a Dutch family and had recently married Edward Doering.*[110]*]*

April 22nd – We went this evening to the theatre, with which I was much surprised and pleased – the performance was Greek and Latin to me *[because it was in Dutch],* nevertheless I was amused. The performers were all amateurs and gentlemen and I had no conception that gents would make such good ladies. I should have had no idea that the female characters were sustained by persons of the masculine gender if I had not previously been informed. The interior of the building is really beautiful, I think in better taste than the generality of our theatres in England; small, of course, a large one would not pay. The only objection to it is that the ladies sit 'like pretty maidens all in a row' and the gents are not allowed the privilege of mixing with them. This they complain of seriously.

April 24th – I accompanied Mr. and Mrs. Doering to the English church, a very small congregation – dined at Mr Roberts' and in the evening took a drive in returning home. I am absolutely enchanted with the neighbourhood of Batavia. I have never yet seen any country so rich and beautiful. If ever fairyland existed surely this must have been the spot. I was delighted with it when I first saw it, but it appears to me to have increased in beauty during our absence. We saw it now in the greatest perfection, the rainy season having the effect of enriching and refurbishing everything so much, and as the fine weather has commenced all the beautiful country residences of which there are a greater number together than in the neighbourhood of any place I have ever been in, are cleaned and whitewashed. The climate also is healthy now; we do not need to fear sickness.

April 25th – A few friends to dinner – in the evening we actually performed an exploit – Mrs. Jutting (the aunt of Mrs. Doering), Mrs D and I, accompanied by Tom, walked round the King's Plain, which is considered to be a distance of three mile. It was a beautiful, cool, moonlit night and we enjoyed our walk exceedingly and also a little bread and butter and a glass of wine after it. Some letters went to England, I wrote a very hasty one to Mrs. Joe Davies, [and] my kind and generous husband made me a present of an elegant little Japan worktable.

April 30th – We entertained a party on board the *Bencoolen*, we sat down to dinner about sixteen or eighteen and our friends seemed to enjoy themselves exceedingly. The day was very favourable, particularly the evening, the moon shone in all its splendour. Tom and I remained on board to make some little arrangements. We returned to Batavia on the next morning and went as usual to dine at Mr. Roberts, being Sunday.

May 2nd – Today I accompanied Mrs. Doering and Mrs. Roberts to a Chinese wedding. If I had the 'pen of a ready writer' I could make a most entertaining story, but unfortunately my talent lies neither in the descriptive nor in the imaginative, but in the stupid *[i.e. comic]*. However, this much I can say, I was excessively amused and gratified at a scene so novel.

The day is spent altogether both by bride and bridegroom in a succession of ceremonials and all the friends of the betrothed are occupied in feasting and amusing themselves. It is the custom of the Chinese not to allow their young females to be seen until the moment they are married so that of them it may really be said they take each other for 'better for worse'. Their ceremonies commence at five o'clock in the morning at which time the bride is dressed most splendidly; her head is covered with jewels and ornaments, which appear insupportably heavy. She has a number of dresses on according to her rank: five, six or seven. The upper one of the female we saw was very pretty … it consisted of a green petticoat beautifully embroidered, and a kind of robe of rich crimson damask. The poor creature, who was obliged to sit all day like a statue in a room suffocatingly warm, filled with the smoke and perfume of incense continually burning seemed almost overpowered by the weight and heat of her equipments. She had a train of little beings constantly fanning her. The meeting between the lady and gentleman usually takes place at five in the evening when the latter is then allowed to raise the veil which conceals or at least shades the beauties of the hitherto unknown fair one. This system of proceeding would not at all meet with my approbation in similar circumstances; I should not like to run into the noose blindfolded.

We partook of some of the refreshments provided on the

occasion such as sweetmeats, cakes, and tea of course. Tea is quite an indispensable at a Chinese meeting. What astonished me as much as anything was to see the whole assemblage, men, women, and children, all with diamonds of such brilliant description upon them in rings, earrings, and various other ornaments, but it is very much the custom here to invest a portion or sometimes the whole of their wealth in diamonds.

May 3ʳᵈ – We attended a ball at the Harmonie *[Assembly Rooms]*, where we saw all the beauty and fashion of Batavia. The assembly rooms are handsome and commodious; indeed the establishment altogether is very fair. We had a most substantial supper; a regular John Bull could scarcely have surpassed it. There was roast and boiled, hot and cold. We returned home at a late hour. *[The words John Bull allude to the British East Company, sometimes known as the John Bull Company and renowned for its lavish entertainment. The Dutch had their own East India Company, known by the initials V.O.C.]*

There was a sale of Japanese goods today, at which my good husband purchased to a most extravagant degree. He and Mr Doering dined out; Mrs D and I were tete a tete all evening. We sent letters to England by the *Fabius*. *[The* Fabius *was an American brig of 236 tons, built in 1791 in Philadelphia.¹¹¹]*

May 14ᵗʰ ...the gentlemen have been very much engaged dining with their friends and sometimes we have taken advantage of their absence to make evening visits. I forgot to mention that on the 29ᵗʰ of April a slight shock of earthquake was felt by many people, I regret to say I was not in the least aware of it, but many of our friends felt it distinctly and tell me they perceived the lamps all shaking and also the chairs upon which they were sitting and experienced a strange sensation of dizziness.

An English frigate the *Wolfe*, arrived in the roads the day after, and the captain said the effect on board was as if the ship had struck upon a rock and so severe that some of the people were thrown from their berths. *[The* Wolfe *was an eighteen-gun sloop under the command of William Hamley.*[112]*She had been dispatched from England to cruise against pirates in the eastern seas.*[113]*]*

May 18th – At six o'clock this morning we set off on an excursion into the country. We had a large roomy old palanquin hired for the purpose. We arrived at Buitenzorg *[Bogor]* about eleven, took a very hearty breakfast, afterwards a siesta, and then dressed and went to take a walk. The palace and grounds appeared to me even much more beautiful and rich than when we first visited them in November. Dined late and in the evening, again walked, having the advantage of a brilliant moon.

May 19th – We proceeded on our journey this morning; we left Buitenzorg between six and seven and soon found ourselves in the midst of a most picturesque, rich and beautiful country. The road from Buitenzorg to Tjanjore, the extent of our travels, is a continued succession of hill and dale. *[The post road was built in 1808 on the order of the Governor.]* In one part it goes over a mountain of I should think at least four thousand feet high, winding through a forest of the most magnificent trees I ever beheld. They clothe the mountain completely to the summit and appear as if they would rear their proud heads to the skies. The views in different parts of the road of the hills and adjacent country are very fine. Raffles says in describing the general appearance of the island

"The traveller can hardly advance five miles inland without feeling a sensible improvement in the atmosphere and climate. As he proceeds, at every step, he breathes a purer air and surveys a brighter scene. At length he reaches the highlands, here the boldest forms of nature are tempered by the rural arts of man; stupendous mountains clothed with abundant harvest, impetuous cataracts tamed to the peasant's will. Here is perpetual verdure; here are tints of the brightest hue. In the hottest season the air retains much of its freshness; in the driest, the innumerable rills and rivulets preserve much of their water. This the mountain farmer directs in endless conduits and canals to irrigate the land, which he has laid out in terraces for its reception; it then descends to the plains and spreads fertility wherever it flows".[114]

In travelling from the low county to the hills we had an opportunity of seeing the paddy or rice fields in almost every stage of cultivation. In some places the green blade just peeping through the soil and in others the luxuriant ear waving like corn in our own little isle. Our mode of travelling to us being strangers was novel and singular. Sometimes we were drawn by horses alone, and occasionally we went at a most alarming speed, our attendant screaming and making hideous noises to frighten the horses into a gallop up the hills. At other times when the elevation was not very considerable we had buffalos yoked with the horses and in going up the principal mountain, the Makonedon, we had only buffalos, six. They have great strength in drawing, they look almost like young elephants. If the country was not so interesting and beautiful it would be a very tedious journey from Buitenzorg to Tjanjore the distance is only thirty-six miles and it occupied us eleven hours to accomplish it. There is no town upon the road where we could stop to refresh ourselves but we stopped in the morning at the house of a Chinaman who we were told frequently entertained travellers "un bon homme". Here we enjoyed a very good breakfast. We were given to understand our friend would not take any money, however, he accepted with pleasure some bottles of wine, beer and brandy, and some white bread, and I suppose our matin meal cost us about five times as much as if we had paid for it. We found it such an expensive breakfast that in returning we adopted the economical plan of providing ourselves with a cold roast fowl, some hard boiled eggs, and some bread; wine, beer, etc, we had already.

With Tjanjore we were much gratified, it is one of the principal residences or native towns. It is of considerable extent both in size and population and built upon such a totally different plan from the towns or villages in any part of Europe that I should have regretted exceedingly not having seen a Javan town. *[Apart from being a scenic excursion, the trip to Tjanjore was probably made because it was a coffee-growing region, and Tom traded in coffee.]*

"All the towns and villages whether large or small are fenced in by strong hedges of bamboo and other quick growing plants. Each hut and dwelling being surrounded by a garden exclusively attached to it. The spot surrounding his simple habitation the cottager considers his peculiar patrimony, and cultivates with peculiar care. The cottages or assemblage of huts that compose the town become thus completely screened from the rays of a searching sun, and are so buried amid the foliage of a luxuriant vegetation that at a small distance no appearance of a human dwelling can be discovered and the residents of a numerous society appears only a verdant grove or clump of evergreens. Nothing can exceed the beauty or the interest which such detached masses of verdure scattered over the face of the country and indicating each the abode of a collection of happy peasantry, add to scenery otherwise rich, whether viewed on the sides of mountains, in the narrow vales, or on the extensive plains." *[Julia is quoting Raffles' History of Java, 1817. She had a copy of this beautifully illustrated book with her on the voyage.]*

Notwithstanding all that our friends told us of the severity of the weather amongst the hills, we found it quite impossible to take any exercise during the day; the evenings and mornings were just agreeably cool. We were surprised to observe, as we travelled along, a quantity of strawberry plants apparently in a very flourishing condition. We were also very much astonished when in bed one night, to hear 'God Save the King' sung by a number of jovial persons. We scarcely expected, when in the interior of Java, to hear our national anthem sung by a party of foreigners.

May 21st – We returned to Buitenzorg where we were met by Mr. and Mrs. Doering and Mr. Watson, who had agreed to join us and spend a few days in the country. Unfortunately in the evening Tom was attacked by a feverish cold, which was very prevalent throughout the island, and was so unwell that we thought it prudent to send for the doctor. He passed a most restless night, but in the morning was much better, only prevented from enjoying the country and the pleasure of his friends' society, as he otherwise would have done. Almost everybody, gentle and simple, is attacked by the same kind of illness, though generally speaking I do not think quite so severely as Tom.

12

Clapped in Irons!

May 23rd – Mrs. Doering and I accompanied by Mr. Watson and Mr. Ritchie (Tom was not sufficiently well, and Mr. Doering was too lazy) actually performed a feat. We walked about seven miles before breakfast. Such a thing I suppose was never before accomplished by a lady in this part of the world. We did ample justice to the broiled fowl and potatoes after it, and then to renew our appetite for dinner we passed the morning playing billiards. It was originally intended that we should return to Batavia on the next morning, the 24th, but the moon being so bright offered a great inducement to travel in the evening rather than during the heat of the sun, accordingly about five o'clock we ordered horses and returned after enjoying our excursion into the interior exceedingly. I must confess when we returned home I felt a little fatigued by the exertions of the day and made all possible haste into Bedfordshire.

A most wonderful and extraordinary circumstance happened lately as the *Bencoolen's* boat was returning one morning from the shore to the ship, it and the men in it were attacked by a most enormous monster, a sea serpent as large I suppose at least as any of those prodigies so frequently mentioned by the Americans. Of course, the greatest alarm prevailed, and I know not what fatal consequences would have ensued had not one of the men, with exemplary courage and presence of mind, seized the boat hook and succeeded in forcing it down the throat of the audacious monster, it is still in custody on board of ship and if possible I suppose, will be taken to England to astonish the natives there. I have not yet seen it, but I understand that without exaggeration it is as thick as a man's thigh and twelve feet long. *[This was probably a sea snake; they grow to about five feet long, suggesting that some exaggeration was, in fact, involved.]*

Legendary Sea Serpent

May 26th – During the week there have been several arrivals from various parts and today a long and anxiously expected *Ribble* made her appearance. She left Liverpool on the 10th January and it will scarcely be credited but she had not one single Liverpool paper on board – nor had we one single letter. How to account for it I cannot tell but surely it is most surprising, vessels come direct from England to Manila, Singapore, Batavia, we are in each of these places when they arrive, still never a single line for us. They cannot forget where we are – it cannot be too much trouble for them to write a few lines – what can be the reason? There must be letters I'm sure, but they are directed, for instance, to Singapore when we are at Batavia. We shall certainly get a famous budget some of these days. *[Letters for the Ripleys had been sent to the Cape of Good Hope.]*

June 3rd – I again took leave of all my kind friends in Batavia and embarked expecting to sail on the next morning but some irregularity at the customhouse prevented our departure until the 5th. I could not help feeling a degree of regret at parting from friends whom perhaps I should never see more, and from whom we had received the greatest hospitality and kindness. On the 4th I was much occupied on board having our cabins cleaned and arranged for after an absence of nearly seven weeks I found abundant employment for one day to make all comfortable. The spiders had been most industrious and their airy fabrics were suspended in all directions. Mr. Doering and Mr. Young accompanied Tom on board to take a farewell dinner with us. We were also joined by a Mr. Abeel, a missionary, who had taken his passage in the *Bencoolen* to Singapore. Our friends remained with us until a very early hour on Sunday morning. *[David Abeel was an American missionary who had been working for the Seamen's Friend Society, in 1830 he transferred to the American Board of*

Commissioners for Foreign Missions.[115]*]*

June 5th – Underway at daylight in the morning but a very light wind and poor progress during the day, but at night we had rather severe squalls of wind and rain and on the sixth a tremendous swell of the sea which indeed was so ungallant as to make forcible entry into both our cabins through the stern windows arising in consequence of the extreme depth of the ship. Tom both today and yesterday was very unwell - the effects of the influenza so prevalent in Batavia.

[Abeel was keeping his own journal. Abeel believed that along the western coast of Sumatra 'the pious merchant has it in his power to exert the greatest influence. It is a favorite resort for trading vessels from England and America, and according to the testimony of one who has been engaged in the traffic, the most dishonourable means are often employed in defrauding the natives.'[116]

Whilst some predatory merchants succeeded in exploiting the local people, sometimes the merchants were themselves the prey, and found themselves the victims of pirates. Abeel explains that 'on our way to Singapore we passed a number of islands which are occupied by pirates, who infest the adjacent seas and watch for such vessels as they suppose may be safely and successfully attacked. Three masts generally afford a security, though some ships have been assailed notwithstanding, and those of the crew who remained to tell the tale, with difficulty affected their escape. We saw a number of 'proas' in the Straits of Banka, but either our appearance was too formidable to invite an encounter, or they too peaceful to attack us.' Proas are boats similar to canoes. The Bencoolen may indeed have appeared too formidable, since she was a three-masted ship fitted out with real guns.]

June 12th – Mr. Abeel read prayers and preached to us this morning, we have found him a very mild and gentlemanly young man, an American, and he has taken a great interest in the men, administered both to their souls and bodies, and endeavoured to convince them of the injurious effects of drinking to which they are all so much addicted. I fear however, his preaching will have been in vain for they did not hesitate to tell him they would drink grog whenever they could get it. Perhaps were he to remain longer with us his good advice might be beneficial.

[Grog was an essential part of the average seaman's diet. Although Julia was sceptical about the young missionary's ability to influence the sailors, Abeel felt that he had been quite successful. He wrote that 'the Sabbath was a day of delightful serenity' on board the Bencoolen, *and had given him an opportunity to distribute religious texts. He reported that 'the willingness with which the tracts were received and read by both the passengers and crew afforded a fresh proof of the importance of being always furnished with a supply of these powerful and unobtrusive monitors'. Abeel believed the best way to strike up a good rapport with a ship's crew was to take them seriously; 'a sailor, as all the world knows, is a strange being' he wrote, 'Bluntness is one characteristic, and bluntness mingled with an earnest seriousness must be employed to meet it ... Frequently a shocking oath or loud avowal of their contempt of your presence and purpose are at first employed, by a few of the more hardy spirits to shew to their shipmates their manly superiority to religious scruple ... Let them see that you are doubtless ...and you will generally find these bravados among the most deferential and docile.'*

Significantly, while Abeel was aboard the Bencoolen *there was no crew trouble. As soon as he disembarked in Singapore, problems with the men surfaced again. Thomas Ripley was a man of many talents, but getting on smoothly with his ship's crew was not one of them. Julia was also somewhat critical of the captain and the crew, as the next entry in her journal reveals.]*

June 13ᵗʰ – We passed today exploring new passages – about ten in the morning we were close to the entrance of the Dryon Straits, hoping with a tolerable wind to anchor in the evening at Singapore. By some mismanagement or other, however, the right way was missed and we found ourselves in a passage to which all were strangers. Under such circumstances the greatest caution was necessary, we went with as little sail as possible, but we could not dispense with much for we had a most impetuous current to contend with and although a nice breeze it was difficult to steer the ship through it. It was a dangerous experiment with a vessel so deeply laden, but thanks to our Almighty Protector we got safely through and found it both a very beautiful and a very good channel, we were never in less than nine fathoms of water. Nevertheless I must confess I felt considerably nervous at sailing we knew not where.

I hope a similar occurrence will not happen – we might not a second time be so fortunate but come unexpectedly upon some unseen danger. *[By contrast, Abeel was quite unruffled by this incident, he wrote that the new route 'proved to be a safe and in many respects an advantageous passage'.*¹¹⁷*]*

[That day, Julia writes that she] was much amused with the question of the mate when making his daily observations,

"What shall I call the straits we have been through, sir?"

"Oh! Call them the *Bencoolen's* Straits," was the captain's reply. It seemed that we had got to the eastward of Dryon, and by going the way we did had cut off a considerable corner. The evening became quite calm and we were obliged to anchor about ten miles from our destination.

June 14ᵗʰ – Arrived early in the day at Singapore. *[It was their second visit.]* Tom and Mr Abeel went immediately on shore, and the former returned very soon accompanied by Mr. Diggles, and to my astonishment informed me we should proceed the next day on our voyage. He found no inducement to remain at Singapore. I therefore declined Mr. Diggles invitation to go on shore. We prevailed upon him to take dinner on board, and in the evening were visited by about a dozen of the resident gentlemen who were amusing themselves with boat sailing. *[Was the call at Singapore just to drop off passengers or could it have been to pick up opium? Opium would only form part of the cargo so it could have been taken on board quickly at night. Singapore was quite an emporium for opium.* [118]*]*

June 15th – We weighed anchor about noon, being favoured at that time with a delightful little breeze, which soon took us out of Singapore, I hope for the last time. I think had we remained a few days there we should again have experienced considerable annoyance from the men. *[Many ships used the port of Singapore. There might have been an opportunity for members of the crew of the Bencoolen to jump ship and join another vessel. Thomas thought that he had kept the docile portion of the crew and added to it the Bengalis, hoping that he had stamped out all defiance. The men who remained were well aware of the fate of their shipmates last time they were in Singapore – Thomas had handed them over to the navy press gang. The fact that fresh trouble was brewing indicates that conditions on board the Bencoolen were appalling for the men, who may have been afraid to land smuggled goods in China for fear of being captured and executed.]*

They were completely taken by surprise quitting so soon and had not time to execute any plans which they might have formed previously. But immediately upon departing, three of them refused to work and were put into irons and fed upon bread and water. I strongly suspect they will soon tire of such a mode of living.

June 28th – We sustained a sad loss today, in the death of our little canary. Poor little Dick, he had become so tame that he would even pick biscuit from Tom's lips and he wishing to make better friends with him had put his hand into the cage to take hold of him, when unfortunately the little captive made his escape by some unguarded aperture and flew through the stern window. Tom, with the greatest despatch, had the boat lowered and went in search of the truant and found it, but too late. The fright and fatigue had been too severe for a frame so tender and delicate. Our poor little pet was no more.

June 29th – This evening a strong wind began to blow which continued all night and on the 30th we had a very tempestuous day, hazy and thick and a very heavy sea just such as we had been led to expect the China Sea .... I began to feel timid, I don't know what I shall do in returning home, I think we have been so long accustomed to smooth seas and fine weather that if we have any storms I shall be a great coward. The bad weather was particularly inconvenient today for we were approaching land and could not see more than half a mile before us so that we were close upon the land almost before we could see it. As soon as we could discover what land it was, we found we were about twenty miles to leeward and the night being so unfavourable and the wind contrary, we did not think it prudent to attempt to beat, but came to anchor under shelter of some of the numerous islands by which we were surrounded.

July 1st – About 1 o'clock in the morning the men commenced getting up the anchor, but it was a difficult business. The swell of the sea was very great, the water deep, and the men not in good humour. So that it was a work of at least six hours and when we were ready there was so little wind that during the whole forenoon we scarcely moved through the water. *[Insisting that most of the crew work through the night to raise the anchor was a bad decision. It didn't save any time reaching Macao, and it antagonised the men. Thomas Ripley was impatient and demanding. His actions towards his ship's crew were sometimes tyrannical.]*

Afterwards a breeze sprang up and enabled us to anchor in Macao roads soon after sunset. The scenery, after making the land, was of a very wild character, quite different from any we *[have]* before seen. We were surrounded by an innumerable quantity of islands of the most bleak and barren description I ever saw, not a vestige of vegetation appears upon the thousand rocky eminences which raise their stony heads out of the briny ocean. I do not think the scenery by any means devoid of romantic beauty.

13

China: The Land of Tea

The emperor of China believed that his vast empire could and should be completely self-sufficient. Almost no trade with other nations was allowed at this time. Consequently, with very few exceptions, no foreign merchants could enter Chinese ports. The few merchants who were permitted entry were strictly confined to a row of business premises on the waterfront in Canton (now known as Guangzhou). To make sure that they did not settle in China, they were forbidden to bring their wives and families. Merchants left their families in nearby Macao, a tiny Portuguese colony, leased from China.[119] To establish trade links with China the Ripleys went to Macao to meet their agent, Richard Turner. He was one of only twenty-six British merchants trading in Canton apart from the East India Company's men.[120]

July 2nd – Tom wrote a note early in the morning to a Dutch gentleman requesting him to send a boat to take him on shore, our own little boat not being in very good condition. But it was so long in making its appearance that he lost patience and at two o'clock took the pinnace and sailed away. The vessels are obliged to anchor at a very inconvenient distance from the town – five miles at least. He returned about nine o'clock having delivered his letters of introduction to Mrs. Turner, who kindly offered us accommodation in her house.[121] He met with his friend Mr. Fox[122], in whose company he dined, at the house of Mr Van Basel, the Dutch Consul. He was soon convinced that he was arrived in the land of tea for to his astonishment the gentleman had each a decanter of tea placed at his side during dinner of which they partook instead of wine. Tom could not desert his old friend the juice of the grape, for which he has a much greater respect than for the Chinaman's decoction. *[Although he may not have wanted to drink it, Thomas had a great respect for the profits to be made from tea.]* I must however add that it is not a general custom by any means to substitute tea for wine.

July 3rd – I rose by daylight and prepared to go on shore. About half past seven a large Portuguese sailing boat arrived for our accommodation and at eight we left the ship once more. The first appearance of Macao is rather striking, it is situated completely in a hollow, surrounded on three sides by barren rocks some of which are surmounted by forts by which the town is defended, and which form limits to the liberty of the inhabitants. They look like sentinels exclaiming, "thus far shalt thou go and no farther."

Our *[Portuguese]* boat requiring too much water to land us on the beach, as we approached the shore we were surrounded by a dozen little floating boxes (for I can call them nothing else) managed by women, all crying at the same moment, "Have my boat! Have my boat!" in their broken English. As all seemed to be alike, very neat and clean we made our choice of the one into which we could get the most conveniently. We were much amused with the novelty of the scene altogether. The women were … so much muffled up to protect them from the sun that we could not see them to advantage.

'Little Floating Boxes'

….We were met upon the beach by Mr Fox, who very kindly had his *[sedan]* chair awaiting our arrival to conduct me to Mrs. Turner's. The town is so constructed that the use of carriages is quite impossible and gentlemen as well as ladies are obliged to have recourse to chairs during the heat of the day. It has a very effeminate look but what is to be done? They somewhat resemble our sedan chairs but they are carried higher, upon the men's shoulders, that is to say the poles rest upon the shoulders. I am told that they are much more comfortable than the palanquins of India.

Judging of Macao by the houses which front the sea, a stranger would call it a very respectable place, but every other part of the town is the most abominable I ever beheld. It baffles all my powers of description. The streets are nothing but nasty dirty little alleys – all ascent and declivity – up and down stairs. The pavement is execrable – it seems to me that the planners and builders have been obliged to exert the greatest ingenuity to make it as bad as it is …

We reached Mrs. Turner's house about ten o'clock. Mr. Turner is at Canton, where he, as well as most of the other merchants, lives during nine months of the year quite separated from their wives and families. I cannot imagine a greater sacrifice.

[The Emperor was suspicious of foreigners, who were dubbed 'barbarians'. The Chinese governor of Canton had recently reiterated stern warnings against Europeans " …it has long been strictly interdicted to bring females to Canton… those who come to Canton to trade must yield a trembling obedience to the interdicts of the Celestial Empire".[123] *Three merchants had flouted these restrictions and defiantly taken their wives to Canton. As a reprisal for this and other infringements the Chinese had raided the empty British business premises while the merchants were taking their summer break in Macao.*[124] *This happened just a few weeks before the Ripleys arrived. Thomas could not risk the success of his trading venture by taking Julia further into China. She had to remain in Macao with all the other women.]*

I found the change from our overheated ship to a large, airy, well-furnished house agreeably situated upon a hill with a nice garden, very delightful, and having been up since between four and five o'clock both Tom and I enjoyed our breakfast exceedingly.[125]

… In the evening we took a long walk, we went to one of the boundaries, which I suppose was a distance of a mile and a half. The scenery is really romantic and interesting and reminds

119

me strongly of some parts of Wales. There is an artist here of the name of Chinnery who says every stone is beautiful. *[The well-known artist George Chinnery had a studio in Macao. He made a living painting portraits of merchants and their families. He had come to Macao to escape his wife.[126]]*

Thursday 7th – During the few days we have been in Macao we have received visits from most of the residents. *[One of these was Harriett Low, a young American woman who was keeping a journal of her own. On the 6 July 1831 she wrote 'I thought I would call on the new arrivals and see if it would put me in spirits, called at Mrs Turner's to see Mrs. Ripley, an interesting woman ... '[127]]*

The society is small but very agreeable and good, composed chiefly of the members of the factory and their wives. *[There were about twenty members of the British East India Company based in Canton. The word 'factory' is used here to describe business premises and living accommodation for employees of the EIC.]*

A few of them spent the evening at Mrs. Turner's: Mr. and Mrs. Davis[128] (the next in rank to the chief Mr. Majoribanks[129]), Mr. and Mrs. Thornhill[130], Mr. Vachell the chaplain, Mr. Daniell[131] etc. *[All these guests were top-ranking employees of the British East India Company. Surprisingly, free traders such as the Ripleys and the Turners mixed socially with EIC officials like Majoribanks, even though the EIC was supposed to enjoy a complete monopoly on trade between Britain and China. This was because free traders were needed to bring in the opium that the EIC had grown in India, and the Company then used its opium revenues to buy China tea. The EIC could not risk sending opium directly to China in its own ships because "if the Company were detected importing the drug illegally it would lose its trading rights in China"[132]. In this way the EIC distanced itself from the actual acts of smuggling.]*

120

My dear husband took leave of me about nine o'clock to join the ship, which is to proceed to Lintin in the morning to discharge her cargo. Lintin is about fifteen miles from Macao and ships have the advantage of being much better sheltered there than in the roads of Macao, which are much exposed to the dreadful typhoons prevalent in the China Sea during the months of August, September, and October. Sometimes they are known as early as July. The weather has been very stormy and unsettled lately, I hope however we shall escape one of these awful storms, they resist every obstacle – carry everything before them – not a creature is to be seen whilst the storm is raging, the people are obliged to barricade their doors and windows and sometimes all precautions are unavailing. *[Julia writes this unconvincing explanation in a futile effort to make Lintin sound calm and respectable. In fact it was neither. The shipping roads at Lintin were dangerously exposed. The small mountainous island of Lintin "had been chosen by the opium smugglers as their depot ... where they would be safe under their own guns".*[133] *Any ship that discharged its cargo at Lintin was engaged in smuggling. All legitimate traffic proceeded up the Pearl River Estuary to Whampoa, Canton's official harbour.*[134] *Therefore, Thomas Ripley went to Lintin to smuggle his cargo into China. No details were published of the illicit cargoes that were landed at Lintin so it is not possible to know for certain what Thomas Ripley's cargo contained. There were just a few goods that there was any demand for, these included rice, saltpetre, and opium. By far the biggest demand was for the drug opium. The cargo the* Bencoolen *carried to Lintin may well have included opium, which would have been discharged into a receiving ship at Lintin.*[135] *These were "large armed vessels reposing throughout the year constituting a floating depot of storehouses, for receiving opium in large quantities from the ships bringing it ... and dealing it out in chests and cases to the Chinese junks to be retailed at various points on the shore'.*[136] *British merchants employed Chinese opium buyers to bribe the Chinese officials with 'tea money' or 'squeeze'.]*

I passed a very uncomfortable night being very anxious about the safety of my dear Tom. In the morning, however, Mr. Turner, who I forget to mention arrived at home a few days since, received a note from him to say he had reached the ship in safety about midnight. *[Julia might have been reassured if she had known that vessels 'are seldom interfered with, nor are they likely to be, so long as the free traders can afford to pay the mandarins so much better for not fighting than the government will for doing their duty'.*[137]*]*

July 9th – Mr. Turner left this morning for Lintin and Canton. *[In theory, Chinese regulations prohibited foreign traders from going to Canton between June and September.*[138]*]* Mrs. Turner and I sallied forth to return some visits. We called upon Mrs. Malden, Mrs. Morrison[139], Mrs. Davis, *[and]* Mrs. Lowe. *[Mrs Lowe was American, her husband, William H. Lowe worked for Russell & Co. and Harriett Low was their niece.]*

I like the style of the houses very much, the rooms are so spacious and airy, and they are all furnished with a degree of elegance I have not seen before in the East. The chairs, also, which serve as vehicles possess an excellence in my eyes, which few others may find out. I have no fear of horses running away, nor running over me in the streets, nor carriages breaking down, nor any of those thousand nameless ills to which I feel exposed when making my pedestrian excursions in other towns.

We also visited the studio of Mr Chinnery ... I had heard him so much talked of as an artist of celebrity ... there was a picture which pleased me very much, but it was the production of a Chinese, a copy of Mr C's, a likeness of one of the Hong merchants. *[These were a team of Chinese merchants who alone were allowed to deal with foreigners.]*

Sketch of a Chinese Merchant.

Sunday 10th – We attended the church this morning, which is in the building appropriated to the factory. Mr Vachell the chaplain does not appear to be a man of talent but he gave us a pleasing sermon upon the duty of forgiveness to enemies. *[George Vachell's talents lay in other directions. He was a keen naturalist and sent important specimens to Prof. John Henslowe of Cambridge University. Vachell sent items including dried plants, boxes of insects, edible birds' nests, and the skull of a Chinese mandarin![140] Vachell was courting the attractive Harriett Low, and she describes him as 'her gallant' at this time. However, Vachell was a stickler for punctuality and criticised Harriet and her aunt for arriving late at church. Before long, this and other aspects of his character had offended Harriet, who decided she wished to be 'plagued no more' by him.[141]]*

In the evening we went to Dr. Morrison's, who is fond of collecting friends together on Sunday to prayers and a sermon. During seven months of the year the ladies are left entirely without the benefit of public worship. Mr. Vachell attends the gentlemen when their duties call them to Canton and Dr. Morrison also accompanies them as interpreter; being a very good Chinese scholar *[he had translated the Bible into Chinese]* he has devoted about thirty years of his life to the study of the language and in attempting the work of conversion in which however he has not been in the least successful. He says he does not know of a single instance where his efforts have been effectual. This is somewhat disheartening to those who have and still continue to bestow all their energies upon a work apparently so hopeless, but they are very zealous and await God's own time to crown their efforts with the desired success.

14

Lintin: Haunt of Opium Smugglers

The English which the Chinese talk, is the most extraordinary language I think that ever was heard. I cannot understand them one bit better than if they spoke Latin or Greek and yet they consider their method much more correct than mine. In fact, there are schools established here for teaching them this language, which is considered the very perfection of English. If a lady calls a servant, he invariably answers her 'sir'; I suppose they think there is but one sex … To give a little specimen of their way of talking, Tom wished to make some enquiry respecting the time the ship would be in getting from Macao to Lintin, he was obliged to put the question as follows to have any chance of making himself understood,

"Supposy that pilot boat leave Macao nine o'clock, how soon that boat catchy the ship?"

Answer: "Can catchy twelve clock".

"Supposy that ship leave twelve clock, how long that ship

walky Lintin"

"Can catchy Lintin three clock".

All their language and conversation is in this style, but so pronounced that one cannot distinguish a word scarcely, and they can only understand anyone who speaks to them in this way. *[With very few exceptions, none of the foreign merchants could speak any Chinese. In fact, Chinese regulations governing foreign trade forbade them from learning it in a further attempt to discourage them from settling.*[142]*Some of the merchant's children, however, spoke Chinese.*[143]*]*

Thursday July 12th – We spent a very agreeable evening at Mrs Thornhill's; it was a musical party. *[According to Harriett Low, Mrs Thornhill was 'a pleasant woman ... and has all the open frankness of manner belonging to the Irish character; enthusiastic, affectionate and hospitable'.*[144]*]*

My dear husband arrived in Canton after spending four days very agreeably at Lintin … in the company of several of the factory gentlemen.

July 16th – We went this evening to visit Mr Beale's garden and aviary. He has some beautiful birds and amongst the number, one which is rarely seen alive except in its free and wild state – a bird of paradise – but it was moulting, and had not a vestige of the beautiful plumage which we see brought to England. It is a much larger bird than I imagined it. *[Thomas Beale had been the senior partner in Magniac & Co., forerunner of the famous Jardine, Matheson & Co., but he was fired after a dispute concerning the sale of opium. So there he sat, in a handsome house, with the aviary and the bird of paradise, and not enough money to get back to England.*[145]*]*

July 21st –we have been very dissipated, by which I mean that for the last four nights we have been out to tea every night.

Monday – Mrs. Allport's[146], who lives the life of a recluse – Tuesday – Mr. Robinson's, one of the factory gentlemen *[George Best Robinson was serving below the EIC select committee[147] This apparently unambitious man was at his happiest when spending time at home with his wife and children[148], yet by a twist of fate, he would be rapidly promoted during the next few years and as Sir George Best Robinson, he would find himself in charge when the small British community stood on the brink of the first Opium War.[149]]* Wednesday – Mr. Davis – and Thursday – at the chief's, Mr Majoribanks, where all the beauty and fashion of Macao was assembled – a very pleasant party. I have never met with greater kindness and hospitality in my life than during my visit to this place. I have heard frequently from my husband during his absence and he seems equally pleased with his reception in Canton. Mr Majoribanks this evening paid me very marked attention. *[It was very flattering to Julia that her company was sought by such an important person as Charles Marjoribanks, the EIC's chief representative in China.]*

July 22nd – A large party of us consisting of the Davis', Thornhills, Lows, Mr. and Mrs. Daniell[150], Lindsay[151], etc, etc, took a sail in the evening in the Company's cutter. It was one of the most lovely moonlit nights that could be conceived and having a nice boat and a very agreeable party we all appeared to enjoy ourselves exceedingly. Our object was to land upon one of a group of islands called the Nine Islands about five miles from Macao, where a tent had been pitched and tea and other refreshments provided for us; but upon reaching our destination some of the ladies expressed some degree of apprehension at landing upon unknown ground at night. So a boat was immediately despatched for the provisions, music, etc, for a band had been sent to enliven us whilst rambling about. The party being divided some of course were disappointed at the final determination to remain in the cutter, and I amongst the number. The evening was so delicious and the islands seen by the softening of the lovely moon appeared so tempting and inviting that I could scarcely resist the entreaties of some of the gentlemen to go and take a ramble, but being the only stranger of the party I could not act in opposition to all the rest of the ladies. When the boat returned any eagerness was a little moderated by the mate's description of the place in which the tent had been pitched. He intending to make us sensible of how much we had lost, said a most delightful spot had been fixed upon,

"The grass was quite knee deep."

This satisfied us all, we began to shudder at the idea of snakes and all sorts of venomous reptiles. We soon had some tea made which we found exceedingly refreshing – weighed anchor and bent our way homewards.

We had not a very strong breeze and the tide being completely against us, it was very late ere we reached home, nearly one o'clock in the morning although we had been so short a distance. I enjoyed the evening most exceedingly, but felt a little fatigued after it. Upon reaching my bedroom I found upon the table a most elegant little present *[sent]* from my dear husband – a pair of earrings of most exquisite workmanship.

In the morning I had despatched letters for England by the ship *Hannah*, which was expected to sail in the night. *[The* Hannah, *452 tons, had brought 2248 bales of cotton to China from India*[152]*]*.

July 25th – As I left my room this morning to go to breakfast I was much surprised to be saluted by my dear husband who had that moment arrived having had a much quicker passage than could have been expected from Canton at this season of the year – about forty hours. He was very glad to return having found the heat most intolerable in the capital *[Canton was only a provincial capital, Peking being the capital of China]*. He says he never in any part of the world found the heat so oppressive and intense. He brought me such a 'cargo' of beautiful and useful things of all kinds, that it occupied me the whole day to look at a small part of them.

We spent a very pleasant evening at Mr. Lindsay's, who gave me a set of real Chinese chessmen and a board and promised also to teach me to play the game; otherwise it will be hieroglyphics in England completely. *[Hugh Hamilton Lindsay was the nephew of an earl, described as 'a very pleasant person of courtly and polished manners', who was 'always ready for adventure of any kind'. By October 1833 he had left Macao planning to visit the Pyramids in Egypt.*[153]*]*

July 31st – The whole week has been spent in dissipation. We have been out every evening; Mrs. Grant's, Mr. Majoribanks, Dr. Morrison's, Mr. Daniell's, and this evening it was agreed that we should go and take a sail in the cutter by way of getting a breeze and refreshing us after our fatigues. Accordingly about six o'clock we embarked, but had not gone far before we saw a fast boat approaching with an immense number of oars. All in a moment were upon the qui vive, concluding that it came to announce the arrival of one of the direct ships from England. We made towards it and found all surmises quite correct – the *Waterloo* had arrived after an unusually fine passage of only one hundred days. *[The Waterloo was one of the largest ships in existence, 1325 tons, from the fleet belonging to the EIC.*[154]* To most people, the EIC would have seemed invincible, but as Thomas Ripley stood watching the towering vessel, he was not in awe of this gigantic ship. His huge self-confidence and audacity dared him to plan for a time when he and other free traders would usurp the role of the mighty EIC as suppliers of Britain's tea. It was a prophetic moment.]*

Of course we returned instantly, everyone being so anxious to receive their letters and news from home. It was fortunate that the circumstance occurred for we had scarcely reached the shore before a violent storm commenced which continued for several hours. Captain Roberts came on shore in the morning having arrived the previous evening from Lintin. *[The Bencoolen, under Captain Roberts, may have taken on a new cargo. Tea was the cargo that Thomas Ripley was most interested in acquiring, but this was not the best time of year for buying tea. Furthermore, it was forbidden to import tea into Britain because of the EIC monopoly. If he did buy it, he would have to smuggle it into the UK clandestinely. It is possible that he acquired a cargo of Chinese silk to sell in Manila. We know silk was for sale because officers from the* Waterloo *invested in silk at this time.*[155] *It was one of the officers' privileges to be allowed to carry some cargo on their own account.]*

We continued to enjoy ourselves exceedingly until the 9th of August, on which day we again embarked. I must confess not without considerable regret having never before experienced greater hospitality and kindness in my life. It seems to be the chief object of the residents at Macao to render the sojourn of a stranger agreeable and at this season of the year they have a constant influx and change of society. We continued to receive numerous invitations which of course we were compelled to decline – one a dinner party at the Factory, I should like to have attended. During the gay season it is a weekly meeting …. According to the true John Bull system the ladies form a circle for a little chit chat which in England, and I imagine in Macao also, the gentlemen good-naturedly call scandal – and the gents walk about the veranda amusing themselves pretty much in the same way – and so passes the time away. *[Most if not all of the women were perfectly well aware that opium smuggling was central to the trading concerns of the men at these parties. Julia is very careful not to mention opium in her journal; Harriett Low, however, is much more forthright, and writes about opium trading quite openly.]*[156]

On the 8th of August Tom and I sallied forth in our chairs to bid a final adieu to all the good folks. We had a long list, but we apportioned our visits accordingly and arrived at home again quite in time to make ourselves comfortable for dinner. We were joined at dinner by Mr. Robertson, the partner of Mr. Turner and Mr. Davidson .... In the evening we took a farewell walk accompanied also by Mr.Lindsay, and finished the evening by playing at the scientific game of mouche. *[Mouche is a card game, often played for money.*

Julia left her friends to continue their pleasant lives of parties and social visits. She did not suspect that a few years later these friends and associates would be at the centre of an international crisis that would bring their lives of pleasure in Macao to an abrupt end.]

15

Manila: The Archbishop Enters in Triumph

August 9th – Mr Majoribanks very kindly offered us the use of the cutter to take us bag and baggage on board the *Bencoolen*, too good an offer to be rejected, particularly as by going in it we avoided all the disagreeable*[ness]* of a customs house visa.[157] The morning was wretched, it poured incessantly with rain – a tolerable strong wind and by no means favourable for sailing, however in the afternoon it cleared a little and we said goodbye to our kind hostess Mrs Turner, to whom, particularly as a stranger, I shall always feel much indebted for her attentions. Our sail to the ship in the cutter was most comfortable although the evening was far from being fine. Our friends quitted us between nine and ten, Mr Lindsay leaving with us some very fine tea as a present. I shall be much disappointed if we cannot get it on shore at home as it is of a description that cannot be purchased, and I should like my friends to taste some genuine fine tea. *[A gift of a small quantity of tea would probably be overlooked by British customs.]*

Though I felt some regret at parting from Macao, or rather

the agreeable society I had met with there, I can scarcely express my pleasure at the idea that we were embarking for our homeward voyage. For although in point of actual distance we shall approach home very little by going to Manila, still we were leaving the utmost point of our long extended voyage, and may now really calculate upon every day bringing us nearer to our beloved relatives and friends.

August 10th – At daybreak the anchor was got up but the running was very unfavourable, we beat about for a few hours and got a few miles on our way with the assistance of a little tide, but as soon as that turned against us we could do no good, the sea being very heavy, so we let go the anchor again and tossed about all day in a very uncomfortable manner. I was good for nothing but to loll on the couch.

August 18th – At length the wind has abated and we have now a prospect of reaching Manila in a few days more.

August 21st – This afternoon after a very agreeable passage we arrived safely once more at Manila. We all began to be a little impatient thinking we were long, however, we found other vessels had had more tedious passages even than we had. We anchored about four in the afternoon and I had prepared a bag of clothes hoping to go on shore immediately. We thought we had arrived at a fortunate time, that the doctor and all the other officials would have finished their siesta, and that therefore our visitation would have been over directly. We looked earnestly and in vain for the boat which would grant us liberty to depart. The wind was so boisterous that no boat would venture to the shipping so that we were compelled to make ourselves as comfortable on board as circumstances would permit.

August 22nd – From appearances last night we considered ourselves very fortunate upon arising to find the morning calm and beautiful. At this season of the year it is sometimes not unusual for a strong southwest wind to blow without interruption for a week or even ten days. In which case it is impossible for ships to have any communication with shore. This would have been exceedingly mortifying had it occurred to us. However, Mr. Strachan arrived about eight o'clock …. We received a most hearty welcome from Mrs. Strachan and I am not surprised that she should be delighted to see us for since we left Manila she has been constantly suffering from severe indisposition and has not a single female friend to speak to or render her the little attentions which are so necessary in sickness. The doctor has pronounced her case to be liver complaint and thinks it requisite for her to return to England. She is very unwilling to consent to it, as in all probability her husband will not be able to accompany her.

We found a great change in our old quarters – a division had been put up in the house separating the bachelors and the business entirely from that part occupied by Mr and Mrs Strachan, which makes their abode much more private and retired. *[The house was owned by Strachan, Murray & Co.*[158]*]* We found an excellent breakfast ready which was particularly acceptable after our sail during the day. We saw Mr. Sturgis, Ker, and several of our old friends and usually took a drive after dinner in a pretty little carriage which Mr. Strachan has, capable of accommodating us all, which is more social than the plan we formerly adopted of going in separate vehicles. The country, contrary to our expectations does not look so well, I think, as when we were here before. The foliage perhaps is fresher and greener in consequence of the rains but the fields all look like pools of stagnant water. It is just the season for transplanting the rice and in this state it has no beauty at all. There is a complete scourge of locusts, which is likely to do serious injury to the crops unless some severe gales of wind and rain should come. I am told they are seen in such immense flights that they actually darken the air as they pass. I should like much to see some of them. I suppose they are something similar to the Egyptian plague for wherever they alight they entirely destroy vegetation. *[For nearly three months the locusts had been plaguing Manila, and it was hoped that gales would eventually clear them off.[159]]*

August 29th – Being a great feast day on which no public business is allowed to be transacted, Tom, Mr. Ker and some others made an excursion to the entrance of the lake, just for a little change and shooting. They returned to dinner after having enjoyed themselves much.

Tom is much disappointed to find that permission cannot be obtained from the governor to leave Manila. We had anticipated much pleasure from an excursion to the lake, which is of such immense extent it is almost like an inland sea and surrounded by very lofty mountains and most romantic scenery. But the policy of the government is so narrow that they will not allow foreigners to see the beauties of their country. Many however, take what we call French leave - sometimes they are not molested but they are always liable to be sent back and perhaps kept in confinement for a few days for their temerity – but Tom is determined not to do anything illegally …

September 1st – As usual, took a long drive and concluded it by paying a visit at the doctor, and taking tea there. The wind began to blow and everybody to talk of a colla *[pronounced colia]*, the name by which they designate their severe gales. However, it proved all a false alarm, merely a puff. *[A colla is actually the name of a squall that precedes a gale[160]].*

September 5th – The weather continues very squally and unsettled but neither colla nor typhoon yet. However, it is sufficiently bad to prevent boats from taking cargo to the ships. I hope it will not continue so, otherwise I fear we shall be detained. I received a very nice present from a Spanish gentleman of the name Pereyra *[a Spanish merchant]* of a pair of figures representing the costume of the mestizos of Manila. The dress is so correct and gives such a good idea of the people that I think they will be much admired at home. Wrote despatches for the *Feejee*, which is to sail on the 8th.[161]

September 12th – Whilst we were sitting at tea, one of the boys (for if they are grey-headed old men they are called muchacho) ran into the room to say there was a great fire. The gentlemen immediately took up their hats and proceeded to the direction from whence the flames came. We waited their return with some anxiety fearing lest many poor wretches might have suffered by the devouring element. The loss however fell upon one Chinaman whose sugar manufactory it was. The loss to the poor man was estimated at 10,000 dollars – a sad blow at one stroke. The night fortunately was very fine, there was no wind, otherwise the flames might have spread and the ravage been much worse.

September 14th – A vessel arrived this morning *[the Princess Luisa]* from China bringing news from England to the 6th of May, but very few private letters.[162] Tom received a packet from Mr. Turner from Canton enclosing four numbers of the *Miscellany* for me, all that are yet published, thinking that I had omitted to procure them. It was a Prussian ship and there was a naturalist on board sent by the King of Prussia for scientific purposes. *[This was Hermann von Meyer, the German palaeontologist who was to name and describe several dinosaurs including Archaeopteryx (1861) and Plateosaurus (1837).[163]]* He brought letters from Mr. Strachan to Mr. Lindsay but not speaking English I could not profit by his society. His name is Meyer. The weather has been very wet, stormy and unsettled lately, it has not yet however interfered much with the loading of the vessel. *[The* Bencoolen *took on board a cargo of sugar and hemp.*[164]*]*

September 17th – The *Emerald*, a brig from dear old Liverpool arrived today bringing large despatches to our friends. We of course could not possibly expect letters, but there was a delightful file of *Albions [The* Albion *was a Liverpool newspaper]* which Tom and I devoured very greedily. We did not see any of our immediate connections mentioned in any way, but I regretted to see the death of several acquaintances, amongst others poor Miss Robinson, Mrs. Naegeli's sister, and Mrs Lee, hers is a serious loss leaving so large a family behind her – how truly may we say in the midst of life we are in death. Tom received a letter from Mr. Diggles in which he mentions the melancholy intelligence of the death of several of the young officers whom only a few months back we had seen and known in all the pride of health and youth and enjoying the world as if they thought it their permanent home, little dreaming that in so short a space of time they would be hurried to that world from whence no traveller ever returns. It appears that their regiment the 25th was attacked at Madras or marching up the country, I am not sure which, with cholera, and the ravages it committed were dreadful. Poor Mr. Nichols, Mr. Drought, and Dr. McLeod fell victims. I believe they suffered dreadfully, but a very few hours put an end to their existence and with it all their pains and troubles in this life. *[Ensign Justinian Reynsford Drought of the 25th Madras Native Infantry died of cholera on 28 May 1831. Dr. Donald Ferguson McLeod, a surgeon of the Madras establishment died on the 7 June 1831. However, Ensign Henry James Nichols did not die. He lived another thirty years, and was promoted to Lieutenant in 1832.*[165]*]*

How deficient are we in reflection upon the awful subject of death and eternity when we hear of thousands and ten thousands falling around us, of warnings like these amongst our own acquaintances, a passing exclamation of pity and sorrow escapes us and in a short time we forget almost that such beings ever were…

I was much astonished to see in one of the papers, the marriage of our old friend Mr. Balfour. I thought he would have remained a widower at least a few years longer. I hope he has been successful in his choice of a wife and that it will be in her power to make him more comfortable than the last. I wonder what they think of it in Islington …

September 25th - Our vessel is now ready for sea, but as we do not presumptuously set the weather entirely at defiance, Tom judges it most prudent to remain quietly here until the 10th or 15th of October, as at the end of September when the monsoon is changing there are frequently severe gales and generally very changeable weather. By a delay of a week or ten days it may ensure us a quick and agreeable passage to Singapore – a good omen I hope of our voyage home. *[Another reason for staying may have been to see the Archbishop.]*

September 29th – This morning the Archbishop *[Jose Segui]* made his public entry into the city of Manila after receiving the Pope's Bull ratifying the King's nomination to the high and sacred office.[166] We went to a friend's house to witness the spectacle, which however was devoid of the solemnity we expected. *[The Spanish considered this an occasion for joyous celebration rather than solemnity.]*

Immediately before the city gates an altar was erected at which the right reverend father paid his vows. He then mounted on a white palfrey, gaily caparisoned with silks and gauzes, himself superbly dressed in robes of white satin embroidered with gold, and rode through the principal streets dispensing his blessing to all the people as he passed. The procession ... was commenced by old women dressed as Morris dancers, figuring it away like damsels of fifteen. These were succeeded by bands of Chinese and native music, one following another so immediately that it produced a combination of anything but harmony and sweet sounds. Then came the students of the University – their dresses are very beautiful long robes, some of purple and scarlet, others of green and crimson satin, and lastly came the Archbishop, surrounded by a host of monks and friars ...

The ceremony ended at the Cathedral where everyone endeavoured to get a sprinkle of holy water and a kiss *[of]* the hand of the Archbishop, upon which he wore the magical ring (a splendid ruby), which unites him to his bride, the church. Mrs. Strachan and I were obliged to forego the gratification of witnessing the ceremony at the church, not being aware that we could not be admitted into the church upon a public occasion except in black dresses and with veils thrown over our heads. Tom, however, got the holy father's blessing ...

The day was excessively hot, the sun shone with all his vigour and not being accustomed to be exposed to his midday rays, I felt a little overcome upon returning and was very glad to take a siesta.

October 1st – Another month commenced notwithstanding the monotony of our life here, time flies upon the most rapid wings. We shall soon bid adieu to Manila and commence our voyage for our beloved home. God Almighty grant that it may be safe and prosperous and that we may have a happy meeting with our dear relatives and friends. How I dread finding any blanks I cannot express.

We have become gamblers lately. Three in four evenings when our party has had the addition of a few gentlemen we have amused ourselves with a round game. Winnings and losings have pretty nearly balanced the account.

October 2nd – A dismal day – the gale so long predicted has at last arrived although at present it is not very severe. The rain is coming down in torrents and without ceasing. Mr. Strachan and Tom have been to the bay to see if all the vessels are safe. One, they say, has dragged her anchor considerably but if the wind does not increase I hope she will not sustain any damage.

October 4th – Dined at Dr. Kierulf's and spent a very pleasant day *[Christian Pingel Kierulf and his twin brother, William Duntzfeld Kierulf were Danes who had come to Manila from India.*[167]*]*

On the 6th we had a number of gentlemen to dinner. We played at Speculation in the evening and Tom won a few dollars. In the morning all our *[live]*stock went off to the ship, which looks like a strong indication of our early departure.

October 8th – Tom dined at Mr. Russel's. Mr. Strachan declined going, as it was the last day I should dine with him. Sent Catherine off to the ship in the morning to prepare our cabins.

[Luck was with the Ripleys as usual. Two weeks later a typhoon struck Manila and the brig Emerald, *which had not managed to get away so quickly, was quite severely damaged. She lost her foremast and her bowsprit. The naval vessel the* Crocodile, *which had pressed some of the* Bencoolen's *mutineers, also happened to be in the area. She was caught in the typhoon and suffered damage.*[168]*]*

16

The Hookah and the Monkey

October 9th – About two o'clock we bid adieu to the good old city of Manila and embarked for our own native land, a most delightful feeling …. We were accompanied *[to the ship]* by most of the English residents, who dined on board and did ample justice to our good cheer. They were a merry party, at least if noise constitutes mirth, a merrier never assembled, and certainly if expressions of kindness and wishes for our prosperous and happy return could be availing surely no voyage was ever commenced under more favourable auspices. It was proposed that we should sail about six in the evening, wind permitting, and accordingly a salute was fired about half past five, but at the time appointed it was perfectly calm, so our friends made themselves comfortable for two or three hours longer.

October 16th – We have now been five days at sea and we have not done more than one good day's work. We are little more than two hundred miles from Manila and have a prospect of at least a month's passage to Singapore. The people have been very busy today catching dolphins and trying to catch sharks, but the latter do not appear very hungry, they will not take the bait.

October 23rd .... Our prospect of a tolerable passage is now much more brilliant than it was this time last week. I think there is a probability of our reaching Singapore in five or six days more. *[This would be the Ripleys' third visit to Singapore.]* The island we have passed today is most appropriately named Sapata, which is the Spanish for shoe, to which article we observed a striking resemblance especially to one laced very high above the instep. I forgot to mention our little Manila dog, as mischievous a little puppy as possible. We have given him the noble title of Don. *[Our other dog]* Ben is inclined to be jealous, and with all except his master and mistress I think he has lost a little favour.

October 30th - Almost at our destination, not more than about twenty miles from Singapore, but the ill-natured wind, which seems determined always to thwart us as much as possible is quite contrary, and the chances are very much against our arrival this evening, although it is now only one o'clock. Yesterday we spoke the *Panther*, an American ship which left Manila on the 20th inst. Nine days after us.[169] So that if we had spent another week with our friends in Manila we should have been just as soon in Singapore. Surely we shall make up for all our ill luck by having a fine passage home ... *[The Panther was one of a number of vessels trading out of Rhode Island in the 1830s. She carried cargoes such as cotton, flour, coffee, rice, rum and wine to and from Europe and the East Indies.]*

October 31st – Early this morning we anchored in Singapore roads *[with hemp on board.[170]]*.... The day was very rainy but we did not allow that to prevent our landing. We heard a variety of news from Europe, China, etc, etc. Amongst other things of a dreadful typhoon at Macao, more severe than anything which has been experienced there for many years and unfortunately attended with a serious loss of lives.

I observe by one of the Liverpool papers the death of our old friend Mrs Coulbourn. I cannot say I was much surprised, although her thread of life has been spun out to so great a length that I almost hoped it would have been extended a little longer and that we might have seen her once more. We heard also a most melancholy account of Mrs Lane, or rather her husband, whom she had been so long expecting. He arrived about a fortnight since, quite deranged, and before his departure from England he had taken unto himself "another helpmeet for him" for I think she, poor woman, must have been as mad as he. She was the bosom friend of Mrs Lane and actually had the audacity to write to her and tell her she had been obliged to marry her husband, he would not live without her, but that she might rely upon her taking a very motherly care of her children. Mr L became so violent after his arrival in Singapore that it was found necessary to shave him and put him in confinement. Poor Mrs Lane! I cannot conceive anyone placed in a more distressing situation, to have heard of his death would have been comparative pleasure.

November 1st – 'We take no note of time but as it flies', it cannot fly too rapidly now. I hail the commencement of each succeeding month with delight as bringing me so much nearer to a meeting with my beloved parents and friends *[Only one of Julia's parents was destined to survive until her return]* …

November 2nd – Engaged scribbling a very long chit to Mrs. Strachan to send by His Majesty's ship Challenger, *[commanded by]* Captain Fremantle, which is to sail to China tomorrow … *[Charles Howe Fremantle had recently sailed the Challenger to Western Australia and in May 1829 he had taken formal possession of the whole of the western coast of Australia in the name of King George IV. The city of Fremantle is named after him. The Challenger was a twenty-eight gun naval vessel. In 1835 she was wrecked off the coast of Chile, where 'she was dashed stern first against the rocks on the treacherous Dormido Shoal' (Fitzroy1839). All but two of her crew were saved in a daring rescue headed by Fitzroy, captain of the Beagle, during the voyage when the great naturalist Charles Darwin was on board.]*

November 3rd ... in the afternoon we had a large party of gentlemen to dinner. Whist was the order of the evening. Mr. R won forty dollars. Two or three of the gents indulged themselves in the luxury of the hookah, it is of course considered much more refined than cigars, and there is a style about it - very imposing, but to my plebeian taste it is much more offensive than a simple cigar. The perfume, which is generally thought aromatic, conveys to my olfactory nerves a most medicinal odour ...

November 4th – Some gentlemen to dinner to eat the cold mutton, what they call the brass knocker – whist again in the evening and Mr. R again successful, won forty-eight dollars ...

November 6th – Mr dear father's birthday. What a satisfaction would it be to me could I know that he and my dear mother were alive and well - God Almighty grant that they may be spared to enjoy many happy returns of the day ...

... Dr. Oxley dined with us in the afternoon. *[Thomas Oxley was appointed assistant surgeon to the Residency of Singapore in 1830. He was an employee of the EIC. He owned a plantation in an area south of Orchard Road.]* Received papers from Liverpool to the 27th June by the Gulnare, which sailed from the beginning of July. Each paper that we perused communicates to us the death of some friend or acquaintance, but happily hitherto the 'grim king' seemed to have avoided our own immediate circle. Oh! That he may long pass over those that are near and dear to

144

us…

November 8th – Immediately after breakfast I went on board and was busily engaged all day arranging things for our departure …. *[Meanwhile, the men finished taking on board more cargo, sugar and black pepper.[171]]* Mr R got a most valuable monkey given to him by a Chinaman who had before refused large sums of money for him. Most of the gentlemen in Singapore wished to have purchased him but could not prevail upon the Chinaman to part with him – he is very tame indeed. I hope we may be able to take him home alive, he will require much care when we get into cold weather. We fired a salute at sundown.

November 9th – weighed anchor at daylight, we had very little wind but a strong tide in our favour which enabled us to proceed eight or ten miles. It was too powerful to contend against so that about one o'clock we were obliged to anchor. We had two or three fishing boats alongside, and purchased from them two turtles and some small fish – at six we again proceeded.

…. November 18th – *[Thomas Ripley wanted to return briefly one last time to Batavia to meet with his business associates. He had been considering anchoring the Bencoolen off the northwest end of Java and travelling overland from Anjer to Batavia. Always an opportunist, Tom was delighted when an alternative presented itself.]* At daylight this morning two schooners were in sight and as they were evidently bound to Batavia Tom thought it would be an excellent plan to proceed to that place on one of them rather than go in the ship to Anjer. It would not only save him a little money, a very unpleasant journey of nearly a hundred miles by land, but most probably a day in time, which I look upon under present circumstances as the most valuable of all. Accordingly I rose as speedily as possible and made all his little arrangements for him, amongst other things he did not omit taking with him an excellent supply of food, which he will no doubt find very useful on his return by land, as the accommodation which our own country affords to travellers is not to be met with in this part of the world. His chow chow basket, however, is so amply provided with ham, soup, salmon, chocolate, biscuits, wine, brandy etc, etc, etc, that he might undertake a much longer journey than he is likely to make and not be at any loss for good cheer. *[One wonders how long some of these items would have lasted in a hot climate!]* He left the *Bencoolen* about eight in the morning … *[Tom boarded one of the schooners and then the* Bencoolen *continued making for Anjer with Julia on board.]*

… We certainly ought to be at Anjer tomorrow in good time, for 'The Brothers' are in sight and they are only fifty miles distant from Anjer. I hope we shall arrive safely, since we have lost our 'pilot'. *[Tom was evidently in the habit of overseeing the map-reading and steering of the ship.]* Six o'clock we anchored in a squall of rain and thunder, no wind, about six or eight miles from 'The Brothers', and at eight we were boarded by the officers from a Dutch government schooner, very gentlemanly men. I wrote a few hasty lines to my dear husband, which they politely offered to convey to him, being bound to Batavia where they expected to arrive tomorrow. He will be astonished to receive such an early communication from me. The *Reliance*, the name of the vessel in which he sailed this morning, is said to be the fastest sailer in these seas. I dare say she would not have anchored had she been in our situation this evening.

November 19th – I passed a most restless, sleepless night, dreadfully annoyed by swarms of great cockroaches, and watching for our arrival off 'The Brothers'. We got safely past them about seven in the morning, after beating all night, we had a strong headwind and sea all day and to mend the matter, a current of four knots an hour against us so that our progress has been very inconsiderable, not more, I believe than fifteen to twenty miles. The sea threatened to make forcible entry into my premises in the morning so that I was obliged to send for my friend the carpenter and have one of the deadlights fastened down. I felt a little inclined to squeamishness and in consequence remained in my own cabin alone all day.

November 20th – Still beating away with very little advantage during the whole night, the captain tells me he does not suppose we made a single mile, the weather is thick and rainy also, and consequently is beginning to have a bad effect upon the men. Two of them are laid up today. Surely we shall arrive tomorrow, we are only about fifteen miles from Anjer. I have been amusing myself by writing to Henry in case of a vessel passing for England whilst we are at anchor. I find it very dull being alone in bad weather especially. I shall heartily welcome my dear husband when he returns. I sent Mrs. Doering one of the Manila scarves by Tom, with which I hope she will be pleased, indeed I have little doubt of it, they are so very beautiful. *[Expensive Manila scarves were woven from the fabric of the pineapple, often elaborately embroidered, they were as fine as gauze.172]*

November 22nd – At length we anchored off Anjer and a most tedious time we had, beating about for nearly four days. Anjer is a pretty little village upon a nice sandy beach almost buried in coconut trees and a line of fine bold hills in the background. Last night the current almost drifted us on a dangerous shoal, called the Vrowella Shoal, seven or eight miles from Anjer, so that to avoid it we were obliged to let go our anchor in deep water where we lay quietly until morning, and whilst we were getting underway the master attendant's boat visited us and to my great joy brought me a letter from my dear husband. He arrived at Batavia on the

19th in thirty hours after he left the Bencoolen, and talks of joining us again tomorrow, the 23rd, which I sincerely hope he may do as this is a most exposed road for vessels to lie in during this monsoon. There is not the least shelter from the south and west winds and the sea rolls in with considerable force. The China ships always avoid it on their homeward voyage.

We have been surrounded by native boats bringing poultry, fruit, etc, etc, I have had a feast upon my favourites, mangosteens, I shall not have many opportunities of eating them. The captain *[has]* gone ashore to order our supply of water so that we shall not meet with any detention. How astonishingly cheap poultry is here … what should we think at home of giving one and a half *[old pence]* for a fine fowl? Large turtle at least fifty pounds weight for four shillings. We are pitching and tossing terribly. I hope our good ship will ride safely until her master arrives. I shall be very anxious for the next thirty or forty hours.

17

The Cape of Good Hope: Vineyards and Slavery

November 25th – My dear husband arrived this afternoon after my anxiously expecting him for two days. He left Batavia at seven in the morning and was on board by five in the afternoon, being only ten hours altogether on the road. The distance is about eighty miles. He describes the country as being exceedingly beautiful, in fact the whole island is lovely, it is fertility itself. He brought me good accounts of all our Batavia friends and letters from Mrs. Doering and Mrs. Jutting …

November 26th – This morning at four o'clock to my great joy I heard the cry "All hands up anchor!" and to work they got instantly but unfortunately they had all their work in vain, for when the anchor left the ground, the ship, to use the nautical expression, canted the wrong way and we were too near the shore for her to swing round. We were frightfully near to the rocks, they were obliged to let go the anchor immediately and by assistance from shore they carried a hawser and anchor as far as possible to hold her, then got up the chain, cut the hawser and got safely underway with the loss of anchor and cable, leaving directions however, for it to be given to the *Spartan [another Ripley vessel]* as she passed Anjer. A heavy rolling sea and a lee shore was the cause of our dilemma. However I think if the captain had prudently anchored a mile further from the coast we should have had no difficulty in getting away. It caused us much detention. It was one o'clock ere we had our sails set; we had a strong beating wind. About five, we were alongside an English ship the *Lady Gordon*, bound like ourselves to the Cape. We shall see which makes the best passage. We got considerably ahead before dark.

November 27th – A rough squally night, no appearance of our yesterday's companion, but a brig seen early this morning bound into the straits which we think may very probably be the *Spartan* as she was to leave Liverpool in all July.

December 2nd – Mrs. Pugh's birthday *[Mrs. Pugh was Tom's mother, who had remarried.]* I sincerely hope and trust that she is still in the enjoyment of good health and that she may experience as many returns of her natal day as she can derive any pleasure from. By way of commemoration and, as the evening was dark, we let off a few fireworks, rather a dangerous amusement on board of ship. Poor Jack and Ben *[the dogs]* both exhibit symptoms of greatest horror on these occasions.

December 4th – Eight days since we sailed from Anjer, and we are not more than one good day's sail advanced. We have been as unfortunate as we possibly could, since the 28th we have had very little wind, and that little directly from the quarter in which we wished to go. We must of necessity now have a long passage to the cape. Unless prospects improve I fear my patience will forsake me, it is already beginning to flag …. I have been engaged a part of every day this week in copying letters which Mr R wrote in Batavia.

December 18th – Lat. 15 deg. 49 sec. S. Long. 107 deg. 38-E. I have been so completely out of humour for the last fortnight that to have noted the events of each day would only have been to communicate my own ill temper …. I have been obliged, however, to submit as philosophically as possible to the waywardness of the wind, which has been until yesterday, light and baffling, so much so that we may say that we have only today taken our departure from Java Head, and we expected ere this to have been half way to the Cape. …. I can only attribute my want of patience to my great and increasing anxiety to see my beloved parents, brother and sisters. How my heart yearns to behold them once more! Four months appears to me an interminable space of time … One day is so exactly similar to another that we really "cannot take any note of time but as it flies" and it cannot fly too rapidly.

December 25th - Christmas Day! I can scarcely believe it. There is nothing in the slightest degree to indicate the merry season – no church-going peals, no friendly salutes and congratulations, no blazing fires and joyful parties. The only change in the uniform monotony and dullness of our ship life is that we have had a bottle of champagne and a peacock to dinner, a dish which would have been a little remarkable at a Christmas dinner at home. There is nothing particularly tempting in it; it eats like a tough old turkey. The men too had an extra quantity of currants in their pudding. *[Thomas Ripley's parsimonious attitude towards his crew contrasts sharply with the generosity and hospitality he showed his friends.]*

…How delighted would all the beloved circle at home be if they could but know how comfortable the wanderers are. It would make their hearts more merry consequently, their countenances more cheerful, at least if the wise man's proverb is correct, it would add an additional zest to their Christmas pleasures. I had hoped when we left them to have joined them again long ere this but I sincerely trust this is the last Christmas day I shall ever be absent from them.

January 1st 1832. Another year fled never to return and a new one commenced most inauspiciously.

Calm! Calm! Calm! Oh for a breeze, if it were but a gentle one, to waft us to our beloved home again …. We had hoped to have been at the Cape by the middle of this month – but calculations are entirely out of the question. All that remains is for us to exercise freely all that we possess of that invaluable commodity, patience. The weather has become uncomfortably warm again; we have been obliged to have recourse to our windsail.

January 8th – Lat. 20 deg. 57 sec – S. Long. 66 deg. 40 sec. E. On Monday the 2nd, to our great joy a light breeze sprang up which gradually increased from one to seven knots – so that we have made delightful progress this week and at present there is every appearance of a continuance. During the calm on Monday morning, the sailors caught a fine shark about eight feet long; it was a beautiful graceful creature in the water. It is amusing to see the delight and eagerness with which sailors hook these voracious inhabitants of the deep, although they are too coarse to be eaten with much gout. Still they seem to glory in their destruction as if they were removing from the ocean at least one of man's enemies.

Our cook was afflicted with a slight indisposition for a few days, fortunately no longer, for one day was sufficient to convince us of his importance. Understanding that an excellent substitute had been appointed I sent a case of mock turtle forward to be concocted into soup and anticipated a treat at dinner. Upon tasting it however, to our dismay, we found it had been made with seawater and was totally inedible. Salt is certainly good in moderation, but this far from having lost its savour, was much too savoury. Other things upon the table were scarcely more inviting, so that we all strongly recommended much attention to be paid to our little cook to ensure his speedy recovery. We have another invalid, our monkey Pipes. Tom is attempting to doctor him. I don't know whether he will prove successful – he is such a fine fellow, we shall be sorry to lose him.

January 15th – Lat. 25 deg. 49 sec – S – Long. 50 deg. 48 sec. E. We are making rapid strides each week towards home now: sixteen degrees since last Sunday. On the evening of the 11th, Wednesday, we had strong indications of bad weather, which made us not feel very comfortable as we were in the immediate vicinity of the Mauritius where hurricanes prevail so much at this season of the year or perhaps generally a little later on. As night approached the sea rose ahead and the weather altogether wore a more threatening aspect until about three or four on the morning of the 12th, when it had arrived at a pretty severe gale, and unfortunately not a very favourable one for us. We could just lie our course but were not making more progress than three or four knots per hour. The motion of the ship was most wretched, in all my experience of sea I do not recollect her pitching so much as during the early part of this gale .... Who can conceive the pleasures of a gale except for those who have experienced one? The rolling and pitching, the tumbling and tossing ... the forcible entry of the sea, etc. As to sleep or rest, goodbye to either. To sit up is misery, and to go to bed, I think, is almost worse ....

This evening, the 15th – we were awakened by the captain announcing a sail in sight – we made towards her, spoke her and found her to be a townswoman, the *Harriet*, belonging to Mr Aiken *[of Liverpool]*. She was from Bordeaux, bound to the Isle of

France. *[She]* had been dismasted on the way, and gone to Bahia to repair. She sailed from Bordeaux on the 23rd of September, at which time affairs in Europe were peaceable. Pipes is quite recovered.

.... January 29th – Stormy, variable, uncomfortable weather all week. On the 26th and 27th we were deceived by the appearances of land, which proved on both days to be Cape Flyaway. On the 28th a vessel came up with us (the *Lonach* from Bombay) the sea was too noisy to hold any conversation, but we communicated by means of writing upon boards. *[The Lonarch was 400 tons, almost exactly the same size as the* Bencoolen.*]* It was fortunate that we fell in with her, for the captain corrected our longitude for us, which to our dismay and disappointment was two and a quarter to the eastward of our calculation. It was therefore not surprising that we did not make the land when we expected. It was mutually agreed that we should keep company, both being bound for the Cape. We kept a strong favourable breeze the whole night accompanied by a heavy sea, which this morning struck the ship with such force as to carry a considerable portion of her starboard bulwarks away, which gives us a rather shattered appearance. *[Julia has been at sea so long, that she is almost blasé about the damage to the ship, which sounds substantial.]*

.... January 30th – A very severe contrary gale and heavy sea. No sail set but main and fore topsails close reefed. I think we have not experienced such bad weather since we left England. About six it moderated a good deal and we spoke a brig which had been in sight all day, the *Frances Ann* from Calcutta bound to her port Liverpool, we begged her to report us and were delighted at such a fine opportunity of our friends hearing of us, she will no doubt be at home two or three weeks before us as she does not intend calling at the Cape.

January 31st – A beautiful fine morning, a striking contrast from yesterday. The land was really within sight at daylight and between seven and eight in the morning I went on deck to look at the African shore, we were in Algoa Bay and not more than five or six miles from the land ….

The mate and one of the passengers from the *Lonach* came on board and finding Captain Roberts rather unwell, they very kindly in the course of the day sent their surgeon to visit him. He was accompanied by the *[Lonarch's]* Captain, whose name I did not learn. A most gentlemanly man, such a contrast did the two commanders form! One a finished gentleman in dress and manner, and the other the very picture of a dirty, slovenly, senseless, old woman. I felt actually ashamed of him. *[Roberts may have been following the custom for men to wrap up in shawls when they were ill.]* The weather for the last few days has been pinching cold and we have been obliged to have recourse again to flannels and warm clothing. A nice little fair wind sprang up in the morning and I hope will take us into our port in a very few days.

February 3rd – A fine stiff breeze in the morning and the high land of the Cape descried through the haze, as the sun acquired power it dispelled the mist, and a bold and striking picture was presented to our view, rocks and mountains of the most remarkable forms and character rise in majestic splendour from the ocean bidding defiance to the strong elements. At nine in the morning we were not more than fifteen miles from Cape Town, but unfortunately it became almost calm and we did not anchor until eight in the evening, after being in some time in considerable danger of being drifted upon some terrific breakers – it makes me shudder when I think of the escapes that we have had of being wrecked. If it is possible for us to get into a dangerous position we are sure to find out the way, and of these rocks the captain had been repeatedly warned. I can't tell whether it is ignorance or bravado, which makes him commit such errors, but whatever be the cause, I dread arriving at any port in consequence. *[Although Julia is highly critical of Captain Roberts, he must have been a skilful sailor because he had never been to any of these ports before and negotiated them all successfully.]*

February 4th – Tom went on shore early, but before his departure a young man arrived from his agents Messrs Borradailes, Thompson and Pillans.[173] Of course our own first enquiry was for letters. Oh! We had large packages with orders that if we did not visit the Cape in October they were to be returned and our directions have been attended to. Is it possible to conceive a more severe disappointment? The presence of a stranger scarcely kept me from giving vent to a flood of tears. We had almost lived upon the delightful anticipation of receiving intelligence from our friends. I don't think the mortification would have been half so great if we had been told there had not been any. About one o'clock a young gentleman, Mr Peacock arrived to escort me on shore, a severe south-easter had commenced, which at this season are very frequent; the boatman came to me with a grave and long face and told me it really was not proper for a lady to venture on shore in such a gale. I asked him if there was any danger, he replied he did not think the boat would capsize but I should certainly be wet through, and he was of the opinion that the wind might continue for two or three days. I did not apprehend danger and therefore I enveloped myself in a large boat cloak and took the consequences and after beating about for an hour and a half in not at all an agreeable or enviable way we were safely landed upon the jetty. Catherine *[Julia's maid]* would not be advised before we left the ship to provide herself with a cloak, so that she, as the man predicted, really was wet through. I could not help thinking how dreadfully alarmed my poor mother would have been had she seen me so circumstanced. Tom provided accommodation for us at a boarding house, "Morrison's", which is the usual plan adopted by travellers arriving at Cape Town. We have a private sitting room, but dine at a kind of table d'hote, there is however, only one family here at present: Dr and Mrs Monro, and two daughters, and they appear agreeable people. He is one of the Assistant Surgeons to the colony.

Lieut. Duthie (Mrs Strachan's brother) called in the afternoon and dined and remained in the evening with us, we had some excellent plums and grapes, quite a treat. We took a drive after dinner and had a fine opportunity of seeing the Table Mountain covered with its cloth. It is quite a barometer, a very remarkable phenomenon, but when the south-easters set in they are always indicated by a dense white cloud, which covers the mountain, preserving the form at the same time accurately, and probably no other clouds are to be seen in any direction, which was the case this evening, every other part of the sky was perfectly clear.

February 5th – I was very busily engaged in the morning preparing for the washing. It is extravagantly high here, 3/9 per dozen *[garments]*, but strangers are made to pay for every thing … We took a drive through the town, which is remarkably clean and well built and altogether reminds me more of England than anything I have seen since quitting it. I have been devouring fruit all day. I have not enjoyed anything so much for a great length of time.

February 7th – Mr. Duthie breakfasted with us and accompanied us to the famous vineyard of Constantia, the property of a Dutch gentleman, Mr Cloete. The distance from Cape Town is about twelve or fifteen miles along an excellent road and very diversified and beautiful scenery in many places strikingly similar to what we see in England, but such a show of fruit as Mr Cloete's garden presented I never before beheld and most probably never shall again. It is astonishing how the trees sustain the load under which they labour; the boughs were all weighed to the ground with the largest peaches and pears. I ate blackberries also and the most delicious mulberries I ever tasted, in fact every kind of European fruit grows here in the greatest perfection, of course we tasted all the varieties of Constantia wines, red and white and the grapes from which they are expressed. I prefer the white wine it is very delicious. Tom purchased two small casks of red and one of white. He dined with the officers of the 72nd Highlanders and returned much pleased with his entertainment – everything in excellent style. *[Lieutenant Duthie was a member of the 72nd Highlanders; Tom would have dined as his guest].*

February 8th – Mr Duthie took us to see the museum where there is a splendid collection of birds, chiefly natives of Africa, most of them of brilliant plumage. We dined with Mr Pillans. He resides at a beautiful little cottage about four miles from the town, delightfully situated and quite retired. It was a treat to be a few hours in such a sweet spot for the dust in Cape Town is quite intolerable. I never was in any place where it was so annoying.

February 9th – There was a bazaar held today in the Commercial Rooms, the object of which was to raise money to obtain the freedom of female slaves. *[For eight years before the Ripleys' visit Cape Colony was kept in constant agitation over the issue of slavery. From 1826 slaves could have their freedom bought at a price fixed by an official valuation. Thanks to the efforts of William Wilberforce, slavery was finally abolished in 1834, but former slaves still had to work for their masters for another four to six years.* [174] *]* We strolled into it and were surprised to see such a gay sight there were a great number of very good looking and well dressed ladies we might well have fancied ourselves in England. The Governor, Sir Lowry Cole was there, a fine benevolent looking old gentleman, he is beloved very generally here. We dined at Mr Thompson's and heard that the receipts had been upwards of 100 pounds.

February 12th – It was our intention to have embarked yesterday afternoon, but the south-easter was so strong that we received a message from the ship to say it was impossible to get up the anchor, we bore our disappointment as heroically as possible and this morning at eight o'clock we bid adieu to Cape Town. The contrast to the previous evening was very striking, it was perfectly calm and continued so until noon. I began to fear that we should have no breeze during the day and we all watched for the infallible signs upon the Table Mountain. At length about one o'clock to our great delight we saw a fleecy cloth begin to spread itself and before we were completely underway we had a fine seven-knot breeze. Mr Duthie accompanied us on board and remained until the boatmen warned him that if he waited until the south-easter came he would get completely soaked in returning. We were both much pleased with him; he appeared to be an exceedingly amiable young man and a perfect gentleman.

18

Homeward Bound, Via Napoleon's Tomb

February 19th – What a delightful week. We have had nothing like it since our outward voyage. I suppose we average 160 miles a day since we left the Cape. If our prosperity will but continue a little while we shall soon join our beloved family again.

February 23rd – About eleven o'clock this morning St Helena was descried. Vessels not being allowed to anchor after sunset we unfortunately were just an hour too late and were consequently obliged to lie off and on during the night.

February 24th – We anchored this morning at six o'clock – after a delightful passage of 11 days. What an inhospitable looking island! Poor Napoleon's heart must have sunk within him when he first saw it, although according to Las Cases, when from the deck of the *Northumberland* he surveyed James Town through a spy glass "enclosed as it were in a valley, amid arid and scarped rocks of great height; every platform, every opening, every gorge, bristled with cannon, he did not display the slightest alteration of countenance".[175] *[St. Helena was 'a bastion of black basalt – all that remained of an extinct volcano'.*[176] *Napoleon was taken there in October 1815 and imprisoned by the English at vast expense until his death on the 5 May 1821. He was buried on the island and his simple grave was a tourist attraction until 1840 when his remains were removed and placed in a grand tomb at Les Invalides, Paris.]*

The appearance it presented to the sea is that of the utmost barrenness, yet I believe the valleys are fruitful and picturesque and the climate exceedingly healthy and agreeable. All this, however, or much more could convey little pleasure to a disappointed man whose mighty schemes of ambition were all blighted and who was condemned to perpetual exile from all that he held near and dear to him.

Tom returned in the afternoon after spending a very agreeable *[time]* upon shore, and at six in the evening the men set to work getting up the anchor to my great joy, for every minute's detention appears to me an age. I am so very anxious to set my feet once more upon my own little island. We heard of a dreadful typhoon having taken place in Manila on the 24th of October, very shortly after our departure. Much damage had ensued to the shipping, etc. I am thankful we escaped it. Of course we got an abundant supply of willows from Napoleon's tomb. How they will succeed I cannot guess. *[Tourists liked to take cuttings from the willows surrounding Napoleon's grave to plant in their own gardens.]* We also procured a little fresh fruit, but every article either of necessity or luxury is so dreadfully dear that caution is requisite in giving orders. *[The EIC dominated St Helena, and EIC vessels used the island as a place to pick up water and supplies. The British Navy used it as a base for operations in the South Atlantic.*[177]*]*

February 26th – We are proceeding as delightfully since

our departure from St Helena as before our arrival there. I do not recollect that we have ever during our whole voyage gone so agreeably through the water for a fortnight together as since we left the Cape. I hope it may continue.

March 1st – My dear little Lottie's birthday, God bless her and grant her a long and happy life *[Julia's sister Lottie was fifteen.*[178]*]* At six in the morning the Island of Ascension was visible but at a considerable distance. It was twelve before we were up with it. I suppose we sailed for about two hours along the coast before we arrived at the settlement and we were highly gratified, it is most remarkable land and bears evident symptoms of volcanic origin. It is tolerably elevated, the highest part being between two and three thousand feet above the sea. At two o'clock Tom went on shore to procure some turtle, for which it is so celebrated and returned at five having got three very fine ones. It appears they are government property and the price of them is according to the demand. Ours were valued at 2/10 each, but they receive produce for them instead of money and the barterer is at liberty to put his own price upon his merchandise, so that if a person is not troubled with a very tender conscience he may make them reasonable enough. *[According to the naturalist J. G. Wood the "island of Ascension is a great resort of turtle, which are captured and retained prisoners in some large ponds". Once on board ship they could remain alive without food for about three weeks, and "they were allowed to lie either in the boats or on the after part of the poop, and seldom disturbed themselves unless the vessels gave an extra roll or they were stirred up by having a pail of water thrown over them or a wet swab rubbed over their hooked beaks".*[179]*]*

We were under full sail again with a delightful fresh breeze by six o'clock in the evening, for we did not anchor, we merely lay off and on. We were honoured by the presence of a stranger to dinner, I do not know his name, he was the sailing master of a Brig of War lying at Ascension and a most extraordinary genius he seemed to be. The *Conflict* was the name of the brig.

March 4ᵗʰ The weather continues beautifully fine, but nothing has occurred remarkable since our departure from Ascension. *[Boredom then drove Julia to exchange a bit of scandalous gossip with her maid.]* I cannot resist the inclination I feel to note down a few particulars relative to our noble captain, in consequence of some observations made to me just now by Catherine. His selfishness, penuriousness, and want of cleanliness exceed anything I ever met with before. He has been unwell for the last five or six weeks and during that time has confined himself chiefly to his bed although I think very unnecessarily. Clean linen is universally considered essential to invalids particularly, but it will scarcely be credited that according to the steward's positive affirmation, the captain has never had the linen changed upon his bed since we left Singapore, a period of four months, and a day or two ago since he expressed his astonishment at his sheets being so much soiled and wondered what could possibly be the cause of it. The boy to whom he addressed himself dare not tell him the why and the wherefore, but felt such an irresistible inclination to risibility that he was obliged to leave the cabin. Tom laughed heartily also when he heard it. I believe *[the Captain's]* nightcap is of the same date. Other points in his character are as despicable as his want of cleanliness "take him for all in all I hope ne'er to see his like again". He is truly contemptible.

March 11ᵗʰ – We consider that we have had a most fortunate week having passed from one trade to the other with very little detention, in fact we actually got the N.E. trade in half an hour after losing the S. E. *[The* Bencoolen *had crossed back over the equator.]*

.... a very short time will end our troubles at sea. On the evenings of the 7th and 8th we met vessels, the former we spoke but could not make out her name, she was six weeks from London bound to Batavia. The latter we did not speak as the evening was closing in when we saw her.

Today we had a turtle killed and some soup for dinner; it was remarkable fine.

March 18th – All going on comfortably ... we have had a delightful breeze for the last two days, which has enabled us to lie a better course than before. Today being Henry's birthday we drank his health in a bottle of champagne.

March 25th – Progressed slowly during the week but we have kept fine comfortable weather and it is beginning to be delightfully cool, the thermometer this morning was 68 degrees Fahrenheit.

... We did not forget to drink health and prosperity to dear Charlie today being such a memorable birthday. *[It was his twenty-first. Unlike Julia, Charles never sought prosperity, but he did share her enthusiasm for travel and adventure.]*

April 2nd – Fine strong breezes all week until the 30th of March when we had a dead calm, which was succeeded on the 31st by a severe gale, which continued without intermission until daylight this morning accompanied by a tremendously heavy sea, which made the ship roll dreadfully. I do not recollect our passing two such miserable nights since leaving home. Fortunately we were going before the wind and although unable to carry much sail, having only close-reefed topsails and reefed mainsail, still we approached home about 350 miles in the two days. How delightful and comfortable everything seems after a storm, it is quite impossible for any one to form an idea of it except those who have experienced it. Even today landspeople would think it very rough, but we are delighted at the change from the two previous days. We have seen several vessels this week but have not spoken them. Few people would credit that during the night of the 31st when the gale raged with its greatest fury the Captain never once made his appearance on deck nor gave a single order to his officers respecting the ship. He went to bed as soon as he had dined about four o'clock and did not make his appearance again until eight next morning, breakfast time, when the first question he asked his chief mate was "how in the world the dog Ben had got down into the cabin during the night?" Can he be thought a proper person to have the charge of so many lives and so much valuable property?

April 9th - We have got an obstinate east wind which may detain us no one can tell how long, much longer than I fear than our patience will continue. We met yesterday with a great disappointment: a brig was descried outward bound, she hoisted her number and being at a considerable distance Mr. Ker *[one of the passengers]* mistook the colours and made her out to be the *Ripley*. She was going before the wind and as she did not seem inclined to speak to us a gun was fired of which she took no notice, then another which made her stop, but as we approached her we discovered our mistake and made an apology accordingly to the Captain, which he however did not accept, but told us very unceremoniously he would not have stopped for us if he had not supposed we were in want of something. She was the *Sarah* from Liverpool out ten days.

This morning Tom boarded the *Canada*, one of the New York packet ships, which sailed from Liverpool on the first inst. *[The sailing packet* Canada, *525 tons, was considered to be unequalled when she was launched in 1823. Her dining cabin had polished mahogany tables and sofas and plush crimson draperies.*¹⁸⁰*]* He hoped to have got a file of late papers but only succeeded in procuring one late Liverpool paper and a few London, but as it is said, bad news always travels quickly, he returned with the melancholy intelligence of the sudden death of his brother George. Mr Leather, a gentleman with whom he was slightly acquainted was his informant, but could not give him any particulars except that his death had occurred at Lancaster in an awfully sudden manner whilst attending to his professional duties *[Tom's brother George was a solicitor, he was forty-two at the time of his death.[181]]* Tom was exceedingly shocked and very naturally so. Mr. Leather spoke almost with certainty of my beloved father's existence, but of his continued indisposition.

* * *

I should have continued my journal at least until our arrival in England, which occurred on the 19th of April. We anchored at Cowes, and bid adieu to the ship there, I must even confess with regret, at least as far as I was concerned, for after I had been so long on board I could not help regarding it as my home, and to me "there is no place like home".

The following day we proceeded on to Portsmouth and thence to London where we arrived on the morning of the 21st and hearing the melancholy intelligence of my poor dear father's release from intense and long protracted suffering, we made our stay in the metropolis as short as possible.[182] We left by the mail *[coach]* on the 23rd and arrived in our native place once more on the 24th April 1832. *[The London to Liverpool mail coach departed from the Golden Cross Inn, Charing Cross at 7.30 p.m. and travelled through the night to reach Birkenhead at about 6pm the following evening. Travellers could then take the ferry across the Mersey to reach Liverpool. Mail coaches were lighter than stage coaches, so they usually only carried about four passengers. Every effort was made to shorten the travelling time. Coaches did not stop to pay tolls on turnpike roads; instead the guard sounded his horn to warn the tollgate keeper to open the gates to let the mail through. It was, however, essential to stop at least every twenty-four miles for fresh horses.*

The end of the voyage was the beginning of a new phase of prosperity for the Ripleys. Some of the most exciting events in their lives happened after their return to Liverpool.]

After the voyage 1832 – 1864

$$19$$

Winds of Change

When Thomas and Julia got back home to Liverpool they found huge changes had taken place while they were away at sea. England had a new king, William IV, in whom great hopes for changing the whole political structure of Britain were invested. It also had a new Whig government, committed to change and reform. The country was in the grip of feverish debate about the Reform Bill, for which there was widespread public support.

Thomas and Julia had missed the opening of the Liverpool to Manchester railway in September 1830, and may well have been keen to see it and ride upon it for the first time as thousands of people already had. The impact of the opening of this railway was quite explosive. New businesses had sprung up along the line; the price of transporting goods was coming down. The railway was great news for the business community, of which Tom was such an enthusiastic member. The heyday of the stagecoach was about to come to an end. Already, the railway had snatched the lion's share of the freight and passenger trade between Liverpool and Manchester. Only one stagecoach still ran between the two cities, which people used to send parcels. The L&M was the first intercity passenger railway in Europe, visited by engineers from all over the world – particularly America.

The Locomotive 'Planet' used on the Liverpool to Manchester railway.

People immediately perceived the potential of this new form of transport and the race was on to cover Britain with a network of railways. Sounds of railway construction could even be heard from Thomas and Julia's home in Abercomby Square, which annoyed some of their well-heeled neighbours. One of the residents of this fashionable new suburb wrote a letter of bitter complaint about the noise to the *Liverpool Mercury* in February 1834. Overall though, Liverpudlians were noted for their energetic promotion of the national railway network because of the many positive benefits it brought to Liverpool.

Building the Edge Hill tunnel.
Lancashire Illustrated (1831)

Thomas Ripley's voyage was so successful that on his return to Liverpool he decided to switch from trading with the West Indies to trading with China and the Far East. Thomas had been in partnership with his brother Henry up to this point. There must have been discussions about entering the lucrative trade with China, even though at this time China was not officially open to trade. As soon as Thomas got back the partnership with Henry ended. We do not know if the split was an amicable one. What is clear is that Henry preferred to continue trading with the West Indies. Thomas, on the other hand, was excited by the possibilities of new markets in the Far East.

We know that the two brothers were still in partnership in April 1832 when their ship the *Mary Ann Webb* was listed in the *Liverpool Times* as about to set sail for Calcutta.[183] Six months later the split had obviously occurred; the Liverpool Times no longer refers to T & H Ripley. On the 23rd of October the shipping news tells us that 40 tons of fustic were being unloaded for H.

Ripley. Fustic was used in the cloth industry to produce a fashionable yellow dye. Clearly Henry was continuing to trade on his own. Initially, even after the partnership was dissolved, business was flourishing for Henry. He despatched two ships to the West Indies before the end of 1832: the *Lorten* was entered for loading in November, and the *Matilda* in December.[184]

By 1834 the Liverpool trade directory gives separate business addresses for the two brothers; Henry had an office at 131 Duke Street and Thomas was at 20 Lower Castle Street.[185]

The *Bencoolen*, the ship that Julia Ripley had called her home for almost two years, was laid up. She was in dry dock being refitted at Cowes. The damage sustained on the homeward voyage was so severe that she had to be almost rebuilt. After the extensive work done on the ship she was surveyed at Cowes for insurance purposes.[186] The cargo of sugar and hemp that she had brought home from Manila was reported in the local paper, the *Hampshire Advertiser*, but the hemp failed to command the price that Thomas Ripley was looking for and so he sent it on to America hoping for a better price. However the price of hemp in New York had fallen unexpectedly. "I wish you would let Mr. Ripley know this," wrote merchant Robert Ker, "it may prevent him from suffering further by sending goods to that quarter, which was his intention …".[187]

Meanwhile, the *Bencoolen's* rival the *Meredith*, the ship that had won the race on the outward journey, had met a startling and violent fate on the other side of the world. Like the *Bencoolen*, the *Meredith* was a three-masted ship; she was built in 1827 for the Lancaster firm of Lockerby & Co, and was registered at Liverpool. Three months after the *Bencoolen* limped into port at the end of her journey, the *Meredith* was wrecked in the Hokianga River in New Zealand, far away from the waters in which she usually traded. At the time of the wreck she was still under the command of Tom's rival Captain Fullerton, whom Julia mentions in her journal. Fullerton was one of the survivors. The Australian newspapers reported that the wreck was plundered by local Maori (the indigenous people of New Zealand) who were keen to profit from the catastrophe.

The *Bencoolen* was ready for sea again in January 1833. The *Liverpool Times* reports that she was loading for Ceylon under the command of a new captain, a man named Powell.[188] The Ripleys obviously felt a loss of confidence in Captain Roberts, in spite of the fact that he taken them out to the Far East and brought them safely back - quite a feat in the 1830s. Roberts was ill on the return journey, so it is possible that he was no longer well enough to be captain of any vessel.

Two other ships apart from the *Bencoolen* were entered for loading by Thomas Ripley at Liverpool during the next few months. The ship *James Perkins* set sail for Calcutta in February[189] and the *Spartan*, also for Calcutta, left in April.[190] Henry Ripley was trading with Calcutta too, and his ship the *Mary Ann Webb* was loading for that port in May 1833.[191] She returned in February of the following year with a cargo of rice, saltpetre, ginger, shellac, and sago.[192] Henry's ships even brought back goods from India for other Liverpool merchants. After a fast turnaround, the *Mary Ann Webb* was preparing to return to Calcutta within a month.[193]

While Thomas directed his energy into trade, Julia Ripley took up the threads of her life in Liverpool again. Sociable Julia must have been thrilled to call upon her friends again, and to share with them some of the excitement of her voyage to the Far East. The journal she kept on board ship would have served to remind her of the action-packed business trip that she had undertaken with her husband. However, one of the first things she did on her return was to send her precious journal up to Scotland to a dying woman, thinking that Margaret Duthie might like to read it because it contained news of the son and daughter she would never see again. Mrs. Duthie was the mother of the young lieutenant that the Ripley's had socialised with at the Cape in South Africa, she was also the mother of Julia's friend, Mrs. Strachan (in Manila). In her haste to despatch the journal, Julia simply wrote the woman's address, 11 Charlotte Street, Edinburgh, inside the front cover, and entrusted it to a friend who was travelling up north to Scotland. The postal service was in its infancy, and the mails notoriously unreliable. It was quicker and safer to find someone to take it and deliver it personally.

Time was of the essence, as Margaret Duthie died in October 1832.[194] At the end of her life she was living in a very elegant townhouse in Edinburgh, but she was not a wealthy woman and only had small things to leave her five children. To her son Thomas Duthie, the young lieutenant stationed at the Cape, she left items of silver - things of a convenient size to send out to him in South Africa.[195] Thomas married the following February in the military chapel, and his wife Caroline produced the first of many children later that year.

Julia's friend Mrs. Turner was back in England by May 1832. She had sailed home on the *Bombay*, another of the East India Company's huge ships, (1242 tons).[196] Travelling with her were her four children, Lucy, Richard, Charles and George, and a servant. The family were parted from Mr. Turner who remained in Macao to run his business until the political crisis of 1839 overtook him.

Julia must have been glad to have her own family around her again. In the journal she wrote with regret about not being with them at Christmas time and promised herself 'a double dose of mirth and merriment' when she returned home. Her younger brother Charlie, whose 21st birthday occurred while she was at sea, was a student at Queen's College, Oxford, and received his B.A. in 1834. He got married in May the same year to a woman named Marianne Essex. He then embarked upon a career in the Anglican Church, and in September he was appointed deacon at Lincoln.[197] He didn't stay long in this job, he would soon seek out more exciting opportunities overseas.

Thomas lost another brother in 1834. William Ripley, who also lived in Abercromby Square, died aged forty-five, and left everything to his brother John, who was at that time living in Demerara in the West Indies.[198]

Great changes in the China trade occurred as a result of the East India Company's monopoly ending. This was an event that the Ripleys had been anticipating for some time. The passing of the Reform Act of 1832 gave the industrial towns more of a political voice. This sounded the death knell of the EIC monopoly in China. Free trade with China officially began on 22nd April 1834.

The Ripleys, with their experience as free traders, were poised to take advantage of the change in the law. The *Jumna*, of Liverpool, 364 tons, under the command of Captain J. Pinder, arrived from Canton in March 1835.[199] This was about the quickest that a legitimate trader could return with tea after the change in the law. The vessel belonged to the well-known shipowners T & J Brocklebank, but it was carrying a large quantity of tea for Thomas Ripley. His imports included several varieties of tea, such as bohea, twankey and souchoung. At this time Thomas had to charter some cargo space on vessels belonging to other shipowners because he did not have many ships of his own. His ambitions ran ahead of his available capital.

Although trade with China was now legal for all British

merchants as far as the British Government was concerned, it was not legal as far as the Chinese authorities were concerned. The Chinese were prepared to sell their tea to anyone provided it was paid for with silver. Those in trade were unwilling to do this. It was not advantageous for them. They did not want to send out empty ships, they wanted to trade one commodity for another. The commodity most in demand was opium. Opium was the currency of trade. The drug had to be smuggled in through Lintin, which was not a proper port. The vessels had to moor in the very exposed shipping roads off Lintin, and their contraband cargo was offloaded into 'scrambling crabs' (fast rowing boats with lots of oarsmen).[200] Some of the opium went on shore at Lintin, much of it went into storage vessels, and some was sent up the coast of China in other Chinese vessels, where it also ruined the lives of those who fell prey to the addiction. Of course, European merchants wanted to cut out the middlemen and reap greater profits for themselves by delivering direct to other Chinese ports.[201] Consequently merchants and shipping agents lobbied parliament for the opening of China to trade by force.

Meanwhile in Canton, Sir George Best Robinson was nominally in control of the worsening situation. The Ripleys had met Robinson when they visited Macao before he was promoted. In the autumn of 1835 he wrote "my anxious endeavours will be used for the maintenance of tranquillity," but fearful of the outcome he hid on board the EIC cutter *Louisa*, which was anchored off Lintin.[202] In less threatening times, the Ripleys had enjoyed an evening sailing party on the Company's cutter.

Thomas Ripley knew Lintin well. He had visited it himself, and he had been sending vessels there as 'free traders' for several years. Back in August 1832, the *Spartan* was in the area and was feared lost in freak weather conditions. Merchant James Matheson wrote that 'we had on the 3rd one of the severest typhoons ever known but thank God we have intelligence this morning of the opium ships all being safe. The free trader, *Spartan*…started two hours before it commenced, for Manila and Buenos Ayres, and great fears are naturally entertained as to her safety. She is owned, I believe, by a Mr. Ripley of Liverpool who visited China last year in the *Bencoolen*."[203]

Luckily for Thomas the *Spartan* escaped, and moreover she had been involved in a daring rescue mission; "the *Spartan* is all safe. She was blown out to sea in the typhoon…and returned on the morning of the 6th after having saved the crew of the Java ship, the *Fair Armenian*, which she came up in time to witness foundering".[204] So the *Spartan* had to double back to drop off the crew they had rescued.

Thomas was still using the brig *Spartan* for trade in 1835. In May she was entered for loading for Singapore.[205] She sailed in June under a new captain, a man named Leitch, who replaced her usual captain, Lumsden.[206] Singapore was a port often used for trans-shipping goods, and one of the cargoes frequently transhipped there was opium.[207]

In the same month more tea arrived for Thomas Ripley, on board the *Planter*: 600 chests of tea and two boxes of silk thread, from Canton. The trade with China had been open for little more than a year and already tea prices were falling. In May 1835 the *Liverpool Times* reports a 'fall in price of teas amounts to near two shillings a pound'.[208] This was the result of far greater quantities of tea reaching Britain since the restrictions on imports had been lifted. The tea was also fresher because the EIC used to store it for months in warehouses before selling it.

Business continued to go well for Thomas's brother. Two of Henry Ripley's vessels docked in Liverpool in January 1836.[209]

The *Ripley* brought home a diverse cargo of sugar, rice, caster oil and ginger, as well as rattans, buffalo horns, shellac and saltpetre. The *Mary Ann Webb* had a similar cargo with the addition of a quantity of raw silk to order.

The Goree Warehouses.
Lancashire Illustrated (1831)

Whilst Henry's cargoes had arrived on his *own* ships, Thomas continued to import goods on other shipowners' vessels. The *Esk* brought him seven casks of nutmeg; the *John O'Gaunt* brought tea and raw silk. A further fifteen bales of raw silk arrived for T. Ripley on the *Jumna*. Compared with the quantity of tea he had imported the previous year, these imports were on a relatively small scale. He obviously still thought it was worth trading on this small scale too, although we might guess that his Christmas order of a box of dates and a box of silk was partly for his own family.[210]

The Ripley brothers were enjoying success and wanted to live the lifestyle of wealthy nineteenth century gentlemen. Along with their moneymaking ventures they found time to indulge in the leisure pursuits that they associated with the landed gentry. We know from the journal that Tom enjoyed shooting as a pastime. Henry Ripley evidently enjoyed this sport too. In 1836 he bought a game certificate, for which he paid three and a half guineas, a considerable sum.[211] Henry donated fifty pounds towards a new public hall in Liverpool.[212] The civic buildings of Liverpool reflect the growing wealth of its merchant class during the nineteenth century.

John Ripley, their older brother, had made his fortune in the West Indies and appeared on the social scene in Liverpool at a 'fancy ball' in October, which was held during the music festival. He was dressed, appropriately, as a West Indian planter.[213] A great deal of money was often spent on the costumes for these fancy dress balls, and it was customary to have a new costume made each time by a tailor or dressmaker.

20

Thomas Ripley Meets Lord Palmerston

Merchants at Canton had been expanding their illicit trade in opium for years. In order to evade the Chinese authorities, the opium smugglers continued to use "a convenient opium depot well out in Canton Bay" - the island of Lintin.[214] Its position in mid estuary "was particularly convenient for smugglers of both sides; they could carry away their purchases under cover of night".[215] Because Thomas Ripley's vessels used Lintin, the conclusion has to be drawn that he was involved in smuggling. The question is, *what* was he smuggling? Opium was the most lucrative commodity that could be smuggled into China. Vessels smuggling opium typically made a triangular voyage to Calcutta to pick up opium, on to Lintin to drop it off, returning with tea to their home port.

The *Bencoolen* made this classic triangular trip in 1837. She sailed to Calcutta where there were factories that processed large quantities of opium, which the EIC sold openly at auction.[216] The *Canton Press* records that the *Bencoolen* arrived at Lintin on May the 6th from Calcutta, and her cargo was consigned to Turner

& Co. That year, 1837, it is estimated that British and American opium dealers smuggled 39,000 chests of opium into China.[217] By May the 13th the *Bencoolen* had, presumably, offloaded any contraband and proceeded innocently to the port of Whampoa. She had set sail for Liverpool by the 17th of June. In December she arrived home 'with 1396 bags *[of]* rice from Calcutta, and 1405 packets *[of]* tea from Canton'.[218]

In the same month Henry Ripley also received a cargo from Calcutta on the *Mary Ann Webb*.[219] The crucial difference was that Henry's vessels never made the triangular journey. Henry had no trade with China. He simply traded directly with India, his vessels returned with cargoes of saltpetre, horns, redwood, and other Indian produce.[220] Was Henry too cautious to enter the new trade with China or did his moral principles prevent him? We know that the brothers had very different views on various matters including politics.

A petition protesting about the continued restrictions on the lucrative China trade was presented to Sir Robert Peel by 'merchants and manufacturers of Liverpool, Manchester, *[and]* Leeds' in 1838. The angry merchants had two key demands: they wanted trade with China 'placed on a satisfactory basis' (satisfactory to *them*, that is, but not to the Chinese) and they wanted the government to force the Chinese to lift restrictions on trade in opium.[221] Radical campaigner Richard Cobden was amongst those who signed the petition.

To protect Chinese interests, the Emperor appointed Lin Zexu to the newly created post of High Commissioner in 1838. Unlike other Chinese government officials who had attempted to tackle the opium problem, Lin was energetic and proactive in his efforts to stamp out the illicit trade in opium. Lin believed that the person with overall responsibility for the British was Queen

Victoria. He planned to make an impassioned appeal to her in a letter, explaining that 'there is a class of evil foreigner that makes opium and brings it for sale, tempting fools to destroy themselves, merely in order to reap profit'.[222] Lin wanted to beg the queen for her help in conquering the problem, to urge her to forbid the manufacture of opium in India and to demand that 'what has already been manufactured, Your Majesty must immediately seek out and throw to the bottom of the sea'.[223] There were long delays in getting this letter sent to Britain. It was never received by Queen Victoria.[224] Meanwhile, Lin took action himself. By the spring of 1839 he had arrested sixteen hundred Chinese residents of Canton who were involved in using or selling the drug. He had seized three thousand chests of opium, and confiscated forty-two thousand opium pipes. But so far, he had only taken action against the Chinese, not the foreign merchants.

In March 1839, Lin issued several ultimata. He still refused to deal with the 'barbarians' directly; instead he summoned a meeting of the twelve Hong merchants (the Chinese merchants in charge of dealing with all European trade). The chief of these, at the time, was Wu Bingjiang, known as Howqua. Through them he gave the foreign merchants in China 'an impossible task … within three days somehow, the Hong were to stop a centuries-old enterprise, in particular arrange the delivery of all opium to Lin for confiscation.'[225] At the same time Lin forbade the British merchants to leave China. Howqua gave the orders in person to top merchants such as Dent, Matheson, Green, Daniell, and Wetmore, etc. Some of these men were business associates of Thomas Ripley, or people that he and Julia had socialised with when they were in Canton and Macao. Now, like all the other Europeans in Canton, these personal friends of the Ripleys were involved in an international crisis that soon developed into a hostage situation.

The Europeans still occupied only the small strip of waterfront in Canton where they had their business premises and living quarters. On March 28th 1839 Lin ordered that this area should be sealed off street by street, and guarded by soldiers. The merchants were deprived of their Chinese servants, and since their wives had never been allowed to join them, they had to fend for themselves. In the early nineteenth century, middle-class men were very rarely taught any of the domestic arts, and so it was hardly surprising that, for example, one of them boiled rice to a gluey consistency in an effort to cook a meal.[226] More seriously, Lin refused to allow supplies to be delivered to the hostages, and fears of food shortages spread. At the height of the crisis Thomas Ripley's friend and agent Richard Turner died aged only fifty-three. He died on the 28 March 1839.[227] Another merchant wrote to his sister Harriett Hillard, nee Harriett Low, 'you will have heard of the fate of Mr. Turner, after several weeks *[of suffering]* he died … I believe Mrs. Turner will have your sympathy under this bereavement'.[228]

Charles Elliot, the man sent out from England to deal with the situation in China, had to make vital decisions alone because there was no time to seek the approval of the British Government. He capitulated and ordered the British merchants to surrender all their opium to Lin, promising the merchants that the British government would reimburse them in full. Gradually the other foreign merchants followed suit, and Lin got his opium and took steps to destroy it. By June, Lin had disposed of more than twenty thousand chests of opium and most of the foreign merchants had chosen to flee from the city of Canton.

The situation in China made trade virtually impossible in 1839. Yet in spite of the crisis, Thomas Ripley still managed to import tea. For example, 506 chests of tea arrived rather late in the year, on board the *Tigris*.[229] Astonishingly enough, 1839 was a wonderful year for Thomas. In December, Robert Ker, a business associate, reported 'Ripley in high glee. I have returned from dining with him, he clears £15000 by Coffee, and £25000 by Tea this year, the *Alice Crowther* arrived today with a considerable quantity of Coffee for him ... Tomorrow all well, I ... go to a Ball in the evening with Mr and Mrs Ripley'.[230]

Thomas and Julia were able to afford even more luxuries than before. They continued to acquire expensive furnishings for their house in Abercromby Square. Often these extravagant purchases came from abroad; the *John O'Gaunt* brought a box of paper-hanging for Thomas Ripley.[231] Chinese wallpaper was all the rage at this time amongst the rich. There was a growing interest in exotic imports of various kinds. Smaller luxuries like tea and figs could be afforded by an increasing number of people.

For some Liverpool merchants, 1839 was not such a good year. It had started badly with a furious hurricane in January, which caused a great deal of damage and loss of life both at sea and on shore. Victims of the hurricane who had become homeless or penniless swelled the ranks of the poor in Liverpool, all of whom were dependent on private charity. The Liverpool Shipwreck and Humane Society was founded in response to the catastrophe. Local merchant James Aiken, a personal friend of the Ripleys, was instrumental in setting it up.

The situation in China was deteriorating rapidly. The powerful and wealthy opium merchant William Jardine was back in England from China in 1839. In September he succeeded in meeting Lord Palmerston to discuss military intervention. Jardine reported afterwards that "the extent of armament, number of troops necessary, number of shipping, all were discussed."[232] In an emotional appeal to the British people, politicians Melbourne and Palmerston asserted that the opium Lin had confiscated was not contraband but 'legitimate property'. The merchants who had smuggled it into China were portrayed as 'suffering parties' to whom reparation ought to be made, hence the dispatch of an expeditionary force.[233]

Any Liverpool merchant with interests in the China trade must have waited anxiously for news, which took months to arrive. Thomas and Julia Ripley would have been gravely concerned about the safety of friends in Canton and Macao - people they had dined with, danced with, played cards with - who were now in great danger. Some of the merchants from Canton had fled to Hong Kong, which was at this time 'not a city, but a collection of sleepy fishing villages and a few coves used by pirates'.[234] Rumours spread that Hong Kong might soon be invaded, and Chinese warships were sighted in Hong Kong harbour. Other merchants had returned to their houses and families in Macao. But in August 1839 fears spread that the Chinese wanted to drive the British out of the tiny colony of Macao, which was only leased to the Portuguese. The artist George Chinnery sat gloomily in his studio where Julia had viewed his paintings. Terrified and 'living in the greatest misery', Chinnery predicted disaster: 'Rely on it, something serious if not dreadful is coming … I do not go out again, I think, until I cross the beach' to board a vessel out of Macao.[235] Then the Portuguese governor panicked and ordered all British citizens to leave within twenty-four hours.[236]

Meanwhile, the British government had already despatched naval vessels to the trouble-spot. They wanted to force the Chinese to accept trade on their terms, including trade in opium. The Chinese wanted to prevent this at any cost, because opium had such a destructive influence. As each person succumbed to the drug, his strength would fail, he became 'a walking shadow, eyes vacant, staring. All his powers are consumed in procuring the poison. He becomes a gambler, thief, robber, seldom reaches a very advanced age. Such are the sufferings of millions'.[237]

The governor's order to flee Macao came on the 24th of August; within hours the desperate refugees boarded eighteen ships bound for Kowloon, but bad weather prevented them from leaving port. The next day, the British gunboat, *Volage* (26 guns), arrived at Macao, followed by the fighting ship *Hyacinth* (18 guns).

The British had for years held the high-handed idea that they could win by virtue of their superior naval strength, whilst the Chinese still hoped to expel the 'barbarian devils'.[238] Unfortunately, attempts to find a diplomatic solution were abandoned.

In September, Lin visited Macao to satisfy himself that the British merchants had all left. As was customary, he went about the town in a sedan chair, and Lin was such a large man that eight men were required to lift it. He noted in his diary that the remaining European men '...have heavy beards, much of which they shave, leaving only one curly tuft. Indeed, they do really look like devils'.[239] Having successfully removed the British merchants from Macao, Lin decided the next step was to oust them from Hong Kong. The refugees in Hong Kong were still living on board ship. Chinese warships were preventing the refugees from receiving supplies of food. Charles Elliot then decided to send the *Volage*, the *Louisa*, and the *Pearl*, to attack the Chinese junks. The opening shot was fired by the *Volage* on 3 November 1839. The First Opium War had begun.

Back in London, Thomas Ripley was making sure his voice was heard in the highest places. Thomas and four other merchants from Liverpool had travelled to London that autumn to meet Lord

Palmerston, the Foreign Secretary.[240] At the Foreign Office in Downing Street they discussed the situation in China, and the merchants voiced their concerns. Palmerston said that the matter engaged 'his anxious attention' and spoke of 'the great importance of the trade between Great Britain and China and the necessity of placing it on a more secure footing.'[241] He promised that 'in a few days a Cabinet Council would be held, when the whole question would be considered with the attention its importance demanded.'

Thomas and the others 'left the Foreign Office highly pleased with the manner in which Lord Palmerston had received them, and perfectly satisfied with the assurance that he gave, that in whatever mode the government might deem it necessary to interfere, that interference should be effectual for the protection of the liberties, the lives, and the property of British subjects.'[242]

It is important to remember that the word 'property' alludes to the confiscated opium which British merchants in China had been hoping to make a fat profit on, and 'interference' means war. The British went to war to obtain full compensation for their destroyed opium. Thomas Ripley obviously supported this course of action. By lobbying for more military action, Ripley was guilty of intensifying the hostilities that caused so much loss of life on both sides. Others were bitterly opposed to this. The young politician, William Ewart Gladstone, denounced the war as 'unjust and iniquitous'. Gladstone was disgusted by Lord Palmerston's willingness 'to protect an infamous contraband traffic'.[243] But clearly, Thomas Ripley stood to gain by supporting the war. And gain he did.

The war would last just over two and a half years. Although the ban on trade continued throughout the war many merchants ignored it. Thomas Ripley was one of them. He knew that if he could get ships out there in spite of the ban, he could make a killing financially, and he did.

Opium ships continued to hover off Hong Kong. Twenty-eight trading companies used British vessels as their business premises and living quarters in the absence of a trading base on shore.[244]. They also operated out of Manila, where they offloaded onto Chinese junks, which shipped the drug to the China coast.

In June 1840, at Palmerston's behest, twenty-seven troop ships arrived in Chinese waters bringing three regiments of British soldiers.[245] Despite the military presence, and in defiance of Elliott's ban, trade continued. By November 1840 'forty-three opium ships were using Chusan as an offloading point. Twelve thousand chests of opium, at bargain prices, had been brought through Chusan by the end of the year'.[246]

Manchester Cotton Factories.
Lancashire Illustrated (1831)

Undeterred by the international crisis, Thomas Ripley had recently bought another vessel, the *Litherland*, for use in the tea trade. She was a ship of 305 tons. On the 26th of January 1840, Robert Ker wrote to a business associate MacMicking, in Manila, telling him 'I have been twice to Manchester with Ripley who is now exerting himself to the utmost to despatch the '*Litherland*' his new ship for Singapore and China, failing the latter port she goes to you'.[247]

Anticipating that there might be trouble gaining entry to a Chinese port because of the Opium War, Ker warned MacMicking that the *Litherland* might be diverted to Manila. Thomas planned to base his decision upon the latest news about the war, '*[he]* will write you fully as to the Litherland's voyage, the next overland Mail *[coach]* will enable him to decide'.[248]

In the event, she never went to Manila. Thomas took a calculated risk despatching her to Singapore and Macao under the command of Captain Baxter, and she arrived there in July.[249] She took out a cargo of grey and white shirtings valued at thirty thousand pounds.[250] On the 22 August she sailed from China to Liverpool.[251] She carried 273,876 lbs of tea for the British market, most of it being types of black tea such as Congou and Pekoe. These varieties sold well because the British preferred black tea. Surprisingly, the vessel also carried considerable quantities of green teas, such as Twankay, Hyson, and the variety known by the picturesque name of 'Gunpowder'. It is just possible that Thomas was thinking of trans-shipping the green tea on to America, where there was more of a taste for it.

"Great fortunes making by tea," wrote Robert Ker excitedly in 1840.[252] Ker, in awe of Ripley's phenomenal success, believed that Thomas Ripley was everything a businessman should be. He valued Ripley's net worth in January, 1840: "we may now estimate him £120 to £140,000!!!!!"[253] In 1840 this amount was indeed a substantial fortune.

The Opium War raged on. In 1840 the British had taken Tin-hai on the island of Chusan. News travelled slowly. In Britain as Christmas drew near people were preparing to enjoy the season of peace on earth and goodwill to all men. Then on Christmas Eve the British newspapers reported that Her Majesty's ships *Volage* and *Hyacinth* had engaged thirty Chinese junks, and killed nine hundred Chinese. As a result of this victory, the British were able to erect 'a new fortification' at Hong Kong.[254] This was just the beginning of Britain's historic involvement with Hong Kong that would last over a hundred years, and turned the island into an international business centre.

The following year the *Bencoolen* sailed for Singapore and Hong Kong. Jack Beeching claimed that in the 1840s Hong Kong was 'directly dependant on opium. In Hong Kong it was reported that almost every person of capital not connected with government was employed in the opium trade'.[255] Thomas may have known that he had to use ports other than Macao because of the war. On the 14th of May 1841, the *Bencoolen*, under Captain Caldbeck, arrived safely in Chinese waters from Singapore and Liverpool.[256]

By the end of September 1841 the *Canton General Price Current* - a slender pamphlet at the best of times – ceased publication altogether because of the Opium War. In the very last issue, it was reported that the *Mary Ann Webb* was daily expected from England. Her new owner was *Thomas* Ripley. An important question has to be asked. What had happened to Henry Ripley's business that had forced him to sell his ship? Under what circumstances would a man who had severed his business relationship with his brother have sold his ship to him?

Always ahead of the crowd, Thomas Ripley had been sending ships to Hong Kong since September 1838, when the *Bencoolen* arrived there from Singapore. Her cargo was consigned to Fox Rawson & Company, who had the task of getting the best price for it. Having done so, the agent would also have been responsible for finding a cargo for the return journey. Julia Ripley's journal clearly shows that her husband hated to delegate, and preferred to oversee all business dealings himself. But with a growing business empire and far-flung interests in remote parts of the world, he had to trust his agents' judgement. In 1840, Thomas was furious that an agent had purchased substandard goods on his behalf. There was a bitter correspondence about it: 'Strachan is in great disgrace with Ripley, his Sugar per *Chas Kerr* and *John Renwick* only yields 124 lbs per Picul'.[257] The picul was supposed to weigh about 133 lbs. Thomas demanded compensation, and he got it. His agent, perhaps anxious to keep an important client, backed down, and Ker passed on the news that 'Ripley's claims for deficiency and inferiority to the tune of about eight hundred *[pounds sterling]* have been admitted by Rawson.'[258] By contrast, Ripley was better satisfied with Edward Doering's arrangements for shipping his coffee in 1842. Ker wrote and told him 'I am glad Ripley does not demur at his coffee coming home by the *Tomatin'*.[259] The letter conveys the sense of relief that an agent felt when he had not fallen under the lash of Ripley's displeasure – to borrow Julia Ripley's phrase.

The very same ship, the *Tomatin*, had played an important role in the Ripleys' lives the year before when Julia's younger brother Charlie had set sail for New Zealand. Reverend Charles Lucas Reay offered his services to the Christian Missionary Society in October 1841. The family would have been anxious about Charlie's departure that Christmas, since he was in Plymouth getting ready to set sail on board the *Tomatin*. He embarked on his journey to the other side of the world on Boxing Day, December 1841. He was in good company, since he was travelling with Bishop Selwyn, who was to play a significant role in New Zealand history.[260] It would be two years before Charlie saw his wife and child again.

Like Julia, Charlie wanted to travel. However, the life he went to in New Zealand stands in complete contrast to his sister's experience. She loved luxury, she enjoyed socialising with the elite wherever she was, and she always took an interest in new innovations. On the other side of the world, Charlie started a new life working in remote Maori villages. There were few European settlers in the area around Nelson, in the South Island, where he was based. He preached in barns or in the open air. While Julia was enjoying all the benefits of modernity in her fashionable townhouse in Abercomby Square, Charlie had to put up with primitive conditions and deprivations in his personal life. New Zealander James Stack described Charlie as 'a strong healthy gentleman, capable of enduring much fatigue. He told us what his manner of life is at the South. He goes through thick and thin, comes in gusts of wind on stormy coasts, sleeps often in native huts, eats what providence throws his way amongst the natives, and generally carries his own ... gun to produce food by ... he is a useful, soul-stirring preacher.'[261]

A scandal came to light shortly after Charlie left England. 'After his hurried departure it emerged that he had left debts with local businesses amounting to 105 pounds, 13 shillings and 6 ½ pence. His wife, whom he had left behind at Swanbourne, promised to discharge the debts, but the episode proved deeply embarrassing for those who had arranged Reay's passage under the auspices of the Church Missionary Society.'[262] Why was it that Charlie and Marianne Reay did not receive help from the Ripleys? Was it because Charles feared that the Ripley money had been acquired by immoral means? Many clergymen in England were strongly opposed to the trade in opium. The Church of England had finally been alerted to the situation in 1839 by the Reverend

A. S. Thelwall's publication *The Iniquities of the Opium Trade*.[263] It looks as if a rift may have developed between Julia and her brother that was never healed; Julia would leave nothing to Charlie's family in her will.

21

The Wheel of Fate

Things had gone from bad to worse for Henry Ripley. His shares in the brig *Ripley* were sold in 1840 "for the benefit of his creditors generally".[264] Henry was bankrupt. In a twist of fate, Henry's fortunes had plummeted since the partnership with his brother was dissolved nine years earlier. At the time of the split, Henry had been the more prosperous of the two, a well-established merchant with a solid history of trade with India. Thomas had turned his back on reliable trade to risk everything on a madcap scheme – illegal trade with China. It was a huge financial gamble but it paid off. By 1840 Thomas Ripley's fortune was made and he was already regarded as one of the merchant princes of Liverpool. So when Henry was forced to sell off his assets, Thomas was in a position to buy them. He chose to acquire the vessel *Mary Ann Webb*.

In true Ripley fashion, Henry made a bold attempt to keep trading. He doggedly continued his trade with India by chartering space on vessels belonging to other merchants. On 2 January 1841, the *Thalia* arrived from Calcutta with 217 bags of sugar and 80 chests of shellac for Henry.[265] He was also importing goods from the West Indies again; on the 23 June the *Hebe* arrived from St Domingo, and part of her cargo consisted of mahogany for H. Ripley.[266]

Early in 1841 Henry was out in St Domingo organising his shipments himself. On 20 March he boarded the *Eliza Wylie*, bound for Liverpool.[267] He was on his way home. This was to be his last visit to the West Indies. His wife Mary and his children awaited his return. However, weeks passed and the *Eliza Wylie* did not arrive in Liverpool. Fears mounted as to the fate of the vessel, her crew and passengers. By July, it was feared that she was lost. The discovery of wreckage washed up on the coast of Ireland finally revealed the ship's fate. The *Liverpool Times* reported that some of the broken timbers bore the name *Eliza Wylie*. There were no survivors. The Ripley family now knew that Henry was dead.[268] He was only forty-four years old.

The Duke's Dock, Liverpool.
Lancashire Illustrated (1831)

Thomas had acquired another new role; he had been elected to the Liverpool Docks Committee; it was a prestigious appointment, prized by those with firm ideas for the future of the city. A change of policy by the borough council in 1836 may have enabled Thomas to get this position. It was a change that put more power in the hands of the merchants themselves. The *Liverpool Mercury* reported that 'the power hitherto possessed by the Trustees to revise and annul the proceedings of the Committee [*are*] to be repealed'.[269] By 1837 Thomas was on the Committee where he served conscientiously for many years.[270]

At meetings Thomas often waited silently listening as other members debated the various issues, and then simply cast his vote. Thomas evidently did not believe that he could sway others with the force of his rhetoric. He was a man of action rather than words. This was a key period in the expansion of the Port of Liverpool, and the Docks Committee wielded immense power and commissioned massive projects.

The huge expansion of the Liverpool docks and facilities was necessary because of the fast-growing trade in and out of the port. Business was booming for many Liverpool merchants and Thomas Ripley was amongst the most successful. In February 1841 Captain Freeman docked Ripley's ship the *Litherland* in Prince's Dock, where she unloaded an exotic cargo from China. She brought home silk, tea, and ivory.[271] Thomas insisted on a fast turnaround. In less than three weeks the *Litherland* was entered for loading for Singapore.[272]

Ripley never let the Opium War curtail his relentless pursuit of trade in the Far East. In fact some of his most prosperous years occurred during the Opium War. 1841 was such a year. There had been fighting in and around Canton throughout most of 1841, and because of this the transformation of Hong Kong had begun to take place; by 1842 the city 'was undergoing a metamorphosis into a modern westernised city'.[273] Travis Hanes points out that the transformation was occurring because opium now passed through Hong Kong en route to the mainland.[274]

Shanghai was taken by the British, without bloodshed, on 19 June 1842. In August of the same year, the contentious Treaty of Nanking was signed. Later, the British were permitted to lease Hong Kong, and the island was placed under British Sovereignty. Since Hong Kong was being used for trading opium, many people in Britain who were opposed to the opium trade disapproved of the Treaty. Tory MP Lord Ashley spoke for many when he said, "the peace was as wicked as the war".[275]

The Treaty of Nanking transformed trading patterns with China. Merchants rushed to trade in Canton. So much tea was bought there, that profit margins got smaller and smaller. Jardine, Matheson and Co., an agency whose name was synonymous with opium, had become Thomas Ripley's agents by this time. He wrote to them to explain how he planned to get around the problem: 'whilst I entertain the opinion that little or no good can be done at Canton, a good business will, for a while at least, be carried on to the Northern Ports.' He sent his ship the *Litherland* to Shanghai that year and continued to make plenty of money. He knew that before long, the northern ports would be teeming with merchants, bringing the drug they knew they could sell. 'From what I hear you may calculate on my example being followed,' Ripley wrote, '...not only as regards British Manufactured Goods, but in opium, if the trade should be legalized, as is very confidently expected in this country.'[276] This frank discussion of opium is a clear indication that Ripley was involved in the opium trade and had netted huge profits by pre-empting the legalization of the trade.

Thomas Ripley was doing so well that he planned to set

up his own company in China, and sought out an able businessman from a firm he had dealt with for years, Syme and Co., of Singapore. Charles Shaw, a man Ripley liked and trusted, was chosen to run the new enterprise. Meanwhile, the ship *Liverpool* was sent to China with Ripley's first shipment, worth a staggering £120,000. There were anxieties about insuring the *Liverpool* for her return voyage. The ship was seen as a risk because she was exceptionally large. In one of Ripley's letters to Jardine Matheson and Co., he asserted confidently: 'there is not the slightest difficulty in getting her done here *[in Britain]* and on the very best terms,' since she had always 'delivered her cargo in the very best of order.'[277]

As a result of the fighting and the political turmoil, some businessmen found that life in the Far East was too risky and decided to return to Europe. The Ripleys' friends, Edward Doering and James Strachan both chose to relocate to Britain at this time. Both Doering and Strachan had lived for years in the Far East. They had coped with life in a very different culture and climate. They had run the gauntlet of disease, which took the lives of so many Europeans. Strachan's wife, whom Julia writes about affectionately in her journal, was still in Manila in 1840 but died soon after.[278] She'd been ill for nearly a decade, while James Strachan's work at Strachan, Murray and Co kept him in Manila. By 1842, Strachan was back in Britain, where he lost no time in finding a second wife, a Miss Richardson of Yorkshire.

Edward Doering's family fared better. His wife and children all survived the long voyage to Liverpool in 1841. It was an eventful voyage for Edward's wife Jeanne, who was heavily pregnant when she boarded the ship. She already had three children: eight-year-old John, three-year-old Susanna, and two-year-old Frederick.[279] During the voyage Jeanne went into labour.

Childbirth was risky enough on land in a clean bedroom, attended by a skilled midwife or physician. The ship's doctor was unlikely to have had much experience delivering babies. The provisions would have been poor on a long voyage, with little fresh meat and no fruit or vegetables. The drinking water stored in barrels could become fetid and full of bacteria. This water had to be used sparingly for washing the newborn baby and newly delivered mother. It was little short of a miracle that Jeanne and baby Emma both survived.[280]

The family never went back to the Far East. Doering had been promoted. He returned to Liverpool to take control of his firm's head office.[281] This was a prestigious appointment for Doering, and enabled him to keep his family in considerable style and comfort. In fact, they moved into a house in Abercromby Square, very near to their old friends the Ripleys. When leaving Batavia, Julia had remarked in her journal that she wondered if she would ever see the Doerings again, not realising that they would become her neighbours and that their children would play in the gardens of the square outside her house.[282] Perhaps Julia and Thomas cast wistful glances at their friends' large family, because they were themselves still childless.

It was business as usual for Thomas Ripley in 1842. The new season's tea started arriving in Liverpool in February.[283] Thomas was importing tea in even greater quantities than before. The *Litherland* brought 2,723 chests of tea for him, and a further 1,400 chests for order.[284] She also brought 200 boxes of preserved ginger. Rather later in the season the *Mary Ann Webb*, now under Captain M'Dowal, brought more than 2000 chests of tea and a similar amount for orders. In June, the *Bencoolen* docked in Liverpool, with over six thousand bags of Manila sugar on board and a quantity of sapan wood. She'd also called in at Singapore to

198

pick up nearly two thousand bags of coffee, and a quantity of pepper, and cassia.[285] In October, Ripley received a shipment of 2,201 bags of sugar sent from Manila on board the *Laskar*.[286]

During 1843, while the Treaty of Nanking was being ratified, the tea trade continued to prosper. The *Litherland* returned by 25 April from her annual voyage to China. In addition to her cargo of tea, she carried thirty cases of pongees – a type of silk. In September, the *Liverpool*, an unusually large ship of 962 tons, brought home a cargo of seven thousand chests of tea for Thomas Ripley, one of his largest shipments. Smaller shipments arrived for him on board the *Elvira* in November and the *D'arcy* in December.[287]

In January 1844 the *Mary Ann Webb*, under Captain J. White, was entered for loading for Singapore. Thomas advertised that he had cargo space available on board her. The *Mary Ann Webb* was not a new ship by this time, but she was still in A1 condition, and her hull was coppered and copper fastened.[288] Thomas and his brother had both had years of service from her.

Thomas was now in a position to afford a new ship to add to his fleet. He chose a teak vessel, the *Larpent*, a good-sized ship built in 1843.[289] By December 1844 she was ready for sea. Ripley's pride in his new acquisition saturates his notice in *Gore's Liverpool Advertiser*, when he was seeking to attract passengers and cargo:

'The Larpent … sails remarkably fast and having a large portion of her cargo engaged will meet with quick dispatch. For terms of freight or passage, having splendid poop accommodations, apply to Thomas Ripley."[290]

All the wealthy merchants liked to indulge in conspicuous spending. John Ripley, Thomas' brother, had made his fortune in the West Indies. John had been living in the centre of Liverpool in Canning Street, but in 1844 he acquired a mansion in Wallasey.

The substantial house, which was named Heath Bank, was surrounded by eight acres of grounds.[291] Wallasey was, at that time, quite a rural area, still separated from the city of Liverpool by pleasant country lanes. Thomas and Julia had also set their sights on a country house, and decided upon a property by the sea in the newly fashionable area of Waterloo.[292] It was to become their second home. For two brothers who had grown up in a backstreet pub, the acquisition of this kind of property symbolised their spectacular success.

In 1845 Thomas' trade took a new direction. T & J Brocklebank had found that there was money to be made shipping goods to Australia. The Brocklebanks had a much larger fleet of ships, and Thomas often sought to emulate their methods. Australia was rapidly being colonised by emigrants eager to exploit the rich potential of this new land. The new settlers lacked every type of manufactured goods. Vessels arriving in Sydney Harbour were met by many buyers scrambling for their cargoes. For example, when the *Sarah Birkett* of Liverpool arrived in January 1845 with a cargo of domestic goods, potential customers were warned that 'as all these articles are in great demand, purchasers should make an early application or they will find themselves too late'.[293] The risk and expense of sending a vessel so far was offset by the high prices that the emigrants were prepared to pay. Within the month the *Sarah Birkett*, a tiny brig of 202 tons, was making ready for the long voyage back to Liverpool. An advertisement in the *Sydney Herald* said that the vessel was 'ready to receive cargo' and promised a quick dispatch. Wool was the main export from Australia at this time, it was typically carried at a shilling a bale.[294] Ninety-six bales of wool were stowed on board for Thomas Ripley. In due course, after a voyage of about six months, the cargo arrived safely in Liverpool.[295] He had also made another modest investment in Australian produce, purchasing a quantity of tallow for making candles. It arrived aboard the *Hindoo*, one of the Brocklebanks' clippers, in January of the same year.[296]

It was important to Thomas to look around for new trading opportunities because the tea trade was already becoming more competitive. In Britain, tea imports increased by twenty percent between 1843 and 1845.[297] Duty on tea was still quite high, and stood at more than two shillings per pound weight. Profit margins on tea were relatively narrow. However, Thomas still continued to trade with China. As well as tea, he imported luxury goods: silk and tortoiseshell from Canton in June 1845, and raw silk from Shanghai in October.[298] In three short years since the Opium War ended, Shanghai had been opened up as a trading port and was beginning to eclipse Canton.

In 1845, the bulk of Ripley's other imports came from Singapore, a fast-growing centre for trans-shipping goods. The *St Laurence* brought him black and white pepper in the spring.[299] The *Medina* and the *Dryad* both came in November, bringing him shipments of tin slabs.[300] Thomas also imported seven cases of cigars just in time for Christmas.

22

The Wreck of the *Bencoolen*

The year 1846 opened well, with the exceptionally early arrival of Thomas Ripley's ship *Litherland*, with the new season's tea in January. The earlier the tea arrived, the better the price it would command. The *Shanghae* followed in June with more tea for Thomas and other merchants, which would be sold more cheaply.[301] The *Lena* brought him 171 baskets of mother-of-pearl shells in October. The popularity of mother-of-pearl for decorating ornaments and furniture ensured that this commodity fetched a consistently high price.[302]

Prince Albert's visit to Liverpool in July was the highlight of the year. The main purpose of the visit was to open Albert Dock, but a number of receptions, parties and events were planned so that the 'loyalty of Liverpool' could meet the Prince. As one of Liverpool's successful and wealthy merchants, Thomas Ripley was invited to attend the reception put on by the Dock Committee. Thomas was one of their Vice Presidents. The Mayor spoke for all the merchants when he said that 'the visit of his Royal Highness

… will encourage mercantile speculation and add lustre to mercantile enterprise.'[303] No women were invited to the reception, so Julia was not able to be at her husband's side on this auspicious occasion. She may, however, have been among the 'elegance and fashion of Liverpool', watching the opening of Albert Dock from surrounding platforms, 'provided by the gallantry of the Dock Committee'.

The following day, the Prince laid the foundation stone of the Sailors' Home. Thomas Ripley's friend, James Aiken, was involved in this project, and it was the kind of philanthropic venture that the Prince was keen to encourage. In his speech, Albert said that 'if my visit will assist a work of charity which reflects the greatest credit on your liberality, I shall be glad, for I feel anxious to promote the comfort of those who by their toil and labour, and by exposing themselves to many dangers, contribute to that prosperity which I have this day seen.'[304] Albert's interest in promoting social welfare was avant-garde. Thomas Ripley had not previously shown any concern for the comfort or well being of his seamen. The Prince made this kind of charity both fashionable and patriotic. He even made time for a visit to the Bluecoat School for orphans. This may have been a reason why Thomas and Julia turned their thoughts to founding an orphanage of their own.

Tragedy struck in October. Every day, Thomas was expecting his ship *Bencoolen* to arrive home from Callao. The good ship *Bencoolen*, as Julia called her, had served the Ripleys for nearly twenty years. She had been their floating home throughout their trip to the Far East. She'd voyaged all over the world, calling in at ports in China, India and the Philippines. She was no longer fast enough for the competitive tea trade, which was soon to be dominated by the clipper ships. Instead, Thomas had sent her out to South America for a cargo of raw cotton, hides, and guano.

The *Bencoolen* had made it home safely to the entrance of the Mersey, where she had to wait to take on a pilot to guide her into the Port of Liverpool.[305] It was dark that Saturday night in October, and the wind was blowing a heavy gale. The crew of twenty must have been looking forward to celebrating the end of their voyage in port. Soon they would be paid off, and would, for a moment, have plenty of money to spend. Liverpool had a fine variety of public houses and brothels where they could drink and be merry; places full of song, warmth and companionship. Some of the crew were Liverpool men, and would have had family and friends anxiously waiting for them.

As the *Bencoolen* passed the Formby lighthouse with the pilot at the helm, the ship struck Taylor's Bank, and quickly began to break apart. An order to launch a boat was bellowed above the terrifying noise of shattering timbers. The crew struggled to launch the boat and eight of them scrambled into it. These were the only survivors. The rest of the men, including Captain Claribut, the mates, and the pilot, were tossed into the dark cold water. Even those who could swim would not have lasted long in the cold waves. All thirteen of them drowned.

The morning dawned and the news of the catastrophe spread in Liverpool by word of mouth. It was a Sunday, and since churchgoing was immensely popular in Victorian Britain, the dreadful news would have spread amongst churchgoers like wildfire. There was outrage at the inexplicable loss of the ship and more than half of her crew. She was so near to the port. The pilot was experienced. The weather had been bad, but not so bad that the pilot could not be taken on board. There was a call for an immediate inquiry, and no doubt Thomas Ripley's voice was heard

204

louder than any other.

The inquiry was held in February, four months later. It was to investigate the circumstances of the loss, and also to examine the 'actions and liberal policies of the Liverpool Pilotage Committee'.[306] Shocking evidence emerged. The pilot had been involved in three similar cases in the six preceding years. He had even had his licence revoked for 'gross inattention' to duty. [307] Unluckily for the *Bencoolen*, and for those on board her, the pilot's licence had been returned to him a short time before the fateful night of the wreck.

The boat that saved eight lives was the only one carried by the *Bencoolen*. Julia Ripley called it 'the jolly boat' in her journal, and it is clear that it was the only small boat on board. It was not primarily a lifeboat. It was to be several decades before it was mandatory to carry life-saving equipment on board every ship.

Thomas was able to weather the disaster financially. The *Bencoolen* was insured with Lloyd's, and he owned several other ships. By this time, he had bought the vessel *Old England* for the China trade, and she arrived home in February 1847 with a cargo of tea and silk from Shanghai.[308] Like the *Litherland*, the *Old England* was intended to bring back an annual cargo of tea each spring. The tea that she carried back in February 1848 fetched a good price and sold for about three shillings a pound for the 'mid-quality' tea, showing that tea was still a luxury, to be used sparingly.[309]

Shanghai was still growing in importance as a port at the expense of Canton. Thomas hedged his bets by using *both* ports. At the end of November 1847 the *Grindlay* returned from Canton with nearly two thousand chests of tea.[310]

The sudden death of Julia's brother occurred during 1847. Charles Lucas Reay was only thirty-six when he died in New

Zealand. Charles lived through a time when there was constant conflict between the new settlers who wanted land to farm and the Maori people who were terrified of losing all that was valuable to them. In January 1845 a dispute over land intensified. Sacred trees had been chopped down and houses were set on fire in retaliation. Both sides amassed men to fight and prepared for a battle. Charles Reay wanted to try to prevent bloodshed. He set off with only one other companion, another clergyman, to negotiate with the Maori warriors at their fort. He also met with the European settlers who were armed and ready to attack. He successfully discouraged both sides from confrontation. For this he became a local hero.[311]

On the 2 April 1847 he left Nelson and set out for the North Island to take up a new post, but death overtook him. His wife Marianne and his young son Robert returned to Britain. Although eight-year-old Robert had not been born in New Zealand and had only lived there for about four years, he loved the country and he longed to return.

23

Opportunities in Australia

One brisk windy day in March 1849, the Fitchett family were waiting on a quayside amongst a crowd of people embarking upon the voyage of a lifetime.[312] William Fitchett, his wife Anna, and their five children were emigrating to Australia. The ship was Thomas Ripley's *Larpent*. The Fitchetts must have boarded with some apprehension. To William Fitchett, the ship looked like a giant. The family were leaving everything behind them to make a long and risky journey to the other side of the world on a sailing ship. Their lives depended upon the fate of this vessel and upon the skill of the crew who manned her. On board, the ship was crowded with two hundred and thirty men, women and children. As they were shown below to their accommodation, the Fitchetts would have seen that the vessel had not been purpose-built to carry such a large number of passengers. She had been designed as a cargo ship and had been converted to carry emigrants in a most rudimentary way.

For most passengers, home for the three-month voyage consisted of a long low room in the steerage area with a table down the centre for meals, on either side the sleeping accommodation was arranged in two tiers divided into berths by low wooden planks, each one six foot by six foot, and occupied by four people.[313] For slightly more than the basic fare, small cabins or cubicles were provided below the main deck. There were seven in the Fitchett family, the youngest boy, Frederick, was only a baby; it is very likely that the entire family was crammed into two six-foot berths.

The chance to emigrate had been provided by John Dunmore Lang, a politician and Presbyterian minister based in Sydney. Lang was a colourful individual with woolly unkempt hair and a vituperative personality. He had firm views on the type of immigrant that would most benefit Australia and improve the image of the convict colony. He wanted "to bring out to Australia people whom he thought would make good citizens and were willing to go on the land and farm it".[314] In order to realize his vision, Reverend Lang chartered British vessels. In 1849 the ship he chose was the *Larpent*, owned by Thomas Ripley.

On 30 March the Fitchett family had their last glimpse of England, as the *Larpent* set sail on a voyage that was to last ninety-one days. It was night time as they 'saw for the last time the lights of old England'.[315] Most of the emigrants knew that they would never see England again, and that there was a danger that not everyone on board would live to see Australia, even if the ship did not founder. There was reason for some confidence in the vessel, because the *Larpent* had made the trip to Australia the previous year.[316] However, disease could spread quickly on cramped emigrant ships especially among passengers debilitated by lack of fresh food. Young children were most vulnerable. The Fitchetts had a baby, and four other children aged between three and twelve.

It was a squally passage. In a letter home, William Fitchett recalled watching the sea as a 'high curled mountain billow on the right or on the left *[and]* roll with fearful velocity, and strike her with tremendous force on the 'windward' side shaking our giant ship from stern to stem, making her quiver like a leaf in the wind.' Sometimes he saw 'the furious billow overleap our high bulwarks and sweep the decks and flood the between decks, i.e. our 'houses' and 'bedrooms' … causing the rapid and unbidden movement of pots, bottles, tins, pails and provisions.'[317] In stormy weather like this, many of the emigrants succumbed to seasickness, and Fitchett was, as he delicately puts it, 'surrounded by the eccentricities of our fellow passengers'.

Passenger Acts passed in the 1840s ensured that each migrant had a regular allowance of five pounds of oatmeal a week and another five and a half pounds of food made up of rice, flour, bread or ship's biscuits.[318] They also received two ounces of tea, half a pound of molasses and half a pound of sugar. These provisions sound very meagre, but in fact they represented an improvement on those provided in the 1830s. We know, for example, that Thomas Ripley's crew on the *Bencoolen* had food of a poorer standard. The crew had complained that the food meted out to them was inadequate, even by the standards of the day.

The legislation set out *minimum* standards. However as Blainey explains "on most Australian migrant ships of the 1840s passengers got more than this official dietary scale and also had meat at midday dinner".[319] For the midday meal the usual custom on migrant ships was for the passengers to form themselves into messes of about ten people. The head of the mess collected the cooked meal from the ship's galley and distributed it to the others serving it onto their own plates.

The teatime meal was taken on deck because passengers

brewed their own tea and no cooking was allowed between decks due to the danger of fire. William Fitchett describes how a sudden squall could easily result in "men and women sprawling on the deck", so often one saw "brother and sister at tea holding hands to keep their seat, and holding their tea in the other – teapot, kettle, sugar, bread, butter, spoons, knives and selves too all being sent to leeward if not made taut".[320]

In spite of the fact that the *Larpent* made a relatively quick passage of almost exactly three months, the difficult conditions on board took their toll on the migrants. William Fitchett records that "a fever got amongst the passengers". One by one, the weakest succumbed to the fever. Each time there was a death on board, a burial at sea would be swiftly organised. The latitude and longitude would be noted down in the ship's log, so that the relatives could know the last resting place of their loved one. In all, ten of the people who set out on the *Larpent* died before they reached Australia, and several others were very ill when land was sighted.[321] William himself was one of those who caught the fever and had nothing but a stock of patent medicine known as 'Fawcett's Pills', which he used and fortunately found 'quite sufficient'.

For those who lived to see the new land, it was a very emotional moment. William Fitchett writes that Cape Otway lighthouse was sighted on the evening of 26 June: -

"and a joyous sight it was … every face wore a smile and every heart felt joyful. That sight whilst the air resounded with the loud huzzas, which were repeated again and again by the passengers per *Larpent*. Many a one sat up that night til midnight to see the strange and interesting sights and on the morrow morning had the … sight of being surrounded by land and that land our future home".[322]

The ship anchored safely on 28 June 1849 at Point Henry in Corio Bay. William Fitchett describes it vividly

"The place of anchorage for our ships about seven miles from, but in sight of, Geelong. Highly delighted with the enchanting scenery of this fairy like land. The scenery about Geelong is grand – fair beyond anything I had previously seen or even imagined. The air is clear and strong and the sky wears sometimes the most chaste *[appearance]* and at other times the most gorgeous aspect that could possibly be imagined. The sun has more strength by day, and the moon shines much more brightly by night than in England. Indeed it is not at all difficult to read by the light of the moon."[323]

The Fitchett family felt that their lives had been transformed by going to Australia. William wrote home full of news of the wonderful new life he had made for himself. Keen to impress his relatives back home with the economic buoyancy of the new country, he told them that "most trades are good here". Most of all he was thrilled with the improved standard of living his family were enjoying: -

"I assure you we live well here; and if you were to see us drinking tea three and four times a day, and eating beef steaks for breakfast, and the same or beef steak pie for tea every day, you would think so too. We often wish when feasting ourselves that you were all here to share it, and often talk how Grandfather would enjoy our food, only he would have to give up beast's cheeks and thin end of the breast as well as sheep's heads, for broth is scarcely ever made here – and much as he loves these things he would have to part with them here."[324]

Sadly, William did not live to enjoy all this for long. Perhaps his health had been weakened by the fever he caught on board ship. Although William assured his relatives that he had made a complete recovery, and had been "as well or better than when in England".

Shortly after this letter home was written, he died, and the Fitchett family lost its breadwinner.[325] His wife Anna was left to bring up the family, with the help of income from her oldest son Alfred, who was about thirteen years old. Alfred had a job "in a newspaper office, wages ten shillings per week", as his father had proudly written in his last letter home.[326] Letters such as these were treasured by relatives back in England and inspired further waves of emigrants.

24

The *Panic*: Thomas Ripley's Tea Clipper

Thomas Ripley took the most daring step of his career in 1847. He ordered a brand new tea clipper to be built by Cato, Miller & Co., of Liverpool. Essentially, a clipper ship was built for speed with a slim hull for slicing through the water and tall masts with many sails.

Competition in the tea trade was intense and cutthroat. Paring a few days off the length of the return voyage from China to Britain was crucial. Shipowners and captains would go to any lengths to be the first back with the new season's tea. The vessels needed to be fast sailers. Shipbuilders turned their attention to this and so the famous clipper ships were devised.

Throughout the rest of the century, the clippers came to be icons of the China trade. More and more sails were added to boost the speed to a maximum. Some of these spectacular vessels would become legends in their lifetimes.

Thomas Ripley was a visionary. He foresaw the growing importance of tea clippers. He determined to commission the latest design of vessel. By the mid 1840s a revolution in shipbuilding meant that ships made of iron not wood were now being built. These were still quite rare, but Thomas Ripley was always interested in innovation so he invested in one of the new iron ships. She was a first-class clipper barque, and she was named the *Panic*, implying great speed. In his book *The Tea Clippers*, David R. MacGregor explains that the *Panic* 'must have been one of the earliest examples' as 'not many iron vessels were ever in use in the China trade'.[327] She was a long narrow ship of 400 tons.

Thomas dispatched the Panic to China as soon as she was ready. On her maiden voyage she sailed to Woosung, just north of Shanghai. She arrived on the 17 April 1849, under trusted captain R. F. Howard, a shipmaster who had worked for Ripley before. In September 1849 Howard brought the Panic home to Liverpool with her first cargo of tea.[328] She also brought in a quantity of Chinese silk, 408 bolts for Thomas, and 20 bolts for his friend Henry Killick. The two friends had a reciprocal arrangement for trading and in April 1849 tea and silk for Thomas Ripley arrived on one of Killick's vessels, the Eliza Killick.[329] Another long-standing friend and fellow merchant, Aiken, also carried cargo for Thomas. In May, Aiken's ship the Confucius returned from Shanghai with 95 packages of tea for Thomas amongst her other cargo. Aiken's grown up son had joined him in business, and he now traded as 'J. Aiken and Son'. Thomas had been married to Julia for twenty-five years. They had no children. Thomas was now approaching sixty, and Julia was in her forties. Their childlessness may have been a disappointment to both of them, but it never caused their devotion to each other to waver.

After sending the *Larpent* to Australia twice she was returned to the tea trade. Trading in tea was Thomas Ripley's chief trade, and he had amassed great wealth by pursuing it. In April 1850 the *Larpent* brought back a huge consignment of more than six thousand chests of tea from Shanghai, as well as a quantity of sapan wood. Ripley frequently imported this type of wood; the *Old England* also brought back sapan wood together with hemp and beans when she returned from Manila in January 1850. Sapan wood was used to make a red dye for the textile industry; it could be used to dye silk, cotton and wool.[330]

However, tea was his favourite cargo. The second voyage of the *Panic* was also to China. She picked up tea at Woosung, returned via Anjer, and arrived in London on 10 November 1850.[331]

Concerned about profit margins in the tea trade, Ripley wrote to Lord Palmerston on the subject of assessing duty on tea.[332] For a merchant who imported vast quantities of tea, even a small rise or fall in import duty had quite an impact upon profits. It was very difficult to avoid paying customs duty at British ports, where it was well policed. However, in Shanghai in 1850 "smuggling, or rather non-payment of duty *[was]* becoming more and more the custom … the consul does not interfere in any way in the matter". One merchant boasted to another "we make no entries through the consulate but merely declare what we please and pay what we please to the Chinese Custom House".[333] This lax situation continued for the rest of Thomas's life, no doubt to his advantage.

The affluence of China trade merchants enabled them to finance the building of bigger and better tea-clippers. A new clipper, the *Crisis*, was added to the Brocklebank fleet in 1847. She was built in their own shipyard in Whitehaven. Ripley always envied the Brocklebanks' success, and the *Crisis* was a most successful clipper.

A more famous clipper, the *Reindeer* appeared on the Liverpool waterfront in 1848, and 'attained distinction immediately', by making some very fast passages.[334]

Thomas Ripley's agents managed to secure space on board the *Reindeer* for a cargo of tea in October 1849.[335] The *Reindeer* sailed from the port of Whampoa in China and battled against the southwest monsoon as only a clipper could and reached Liverpool on 19 January 1850. This astonishingly quick passage of only 107 days broke all previous records.[336]

The *Larpent* went missing in the summer of 1851. For months Thomas Ripley would have been unaware of this, because news travelled painfully slowly from the Far East. He would have assumed that she was making her way from port to port. At first her disappearance was unexplained, but in August news of the ship's fate reached the newspapers. According to the report:

"The *Larpent* struck in the night on Cape Formosa, backed off again, filled and went down – leaving those on board barely time to clear away the boats. Six of the sailors took the jolly boat, which was capsized in the surf while attempting to reach the shore. One of them was drowned, being unable to swim – five succeeded in reaching the beach, when they were attacked by the natives, and two of the number cruelly murdered. The surviving three were sold as slaves. The remainder of the crew, including the captain and the mates, started in the long-boat for Hong Kong, and are supposed to have foundered, as they have not been heard of."[337]

In order to raise the money to update to a clipper ship, Thomas Ripley had sold the *Litherland* in 1849. She was bought by a whaling merchant and sailed out to Tasmania to join his fleet. She changed hands again and by 1853 she was supplying goods to the boom towns of the Australian goldrush. On the 18th of June she was returning to Hobart, with a cargo of coal, oranges and bacon. The captain had his wife and four-year-old child on board. The weather was thick and hazy, with heavy showers of rain, when the *Litherland* struck a rock in the Bass Strait. The captain ordered everyone on board to get into the boat, which was hastily cut free from the ship. A minute later the *Litherland* sunk, leaving only the gallant yardarm just visible above the water. The boat was rowed to shore, and everyone landed safely. When they reached Hobart the captain's wife reported, with embarrassment, that the *Litherland* had gone down so quickly that she did not even have time to put on her bonnet.[338]

The wreck of the *Litherland* settled further under the water in a place called Deadman's Gulch. There it lay forgotten in a sandy gully for the next 130 years. In 1983 divers rediscovered the wreckage scattered over fifty metres of seabed. Further surveys were carried out in 1990, and the anchors and a number of ship's timbers were found.[339] These are the only known surviving pieces of any of the vessels that once belonged to Thomas Ripley.

25

Death of a Merchant Prince

By 1851 Thomas had developed heart disease.[340] For a man of such energy and enthusiasm for life this was incredibly frustrating. He found it difficult to slow down. He had no intention of giving up trading while his business was at the height of its success. His brother, John, was retired and living a quiet life as a country gentleman, and Tom's friend Naegeli had moved out to the pleasant suburb of Edge Hill.[341] Thomas wanted to remain at the hub of things; he was totally committed to his work and so for him retirement was not an option. However, he was sufficiently alarmed by the symptoms to ask his solicitor to draw up a will.

Although Thomas had to face his own mortality, he'd always been a risk taker and so he continued to try to live life to the full. During the previous year, he had despatched his tea clipper the *Panic* to Shanghai, and awaited its return with a lucrative cargo.[342] Similarly he had made arrangements to send his ship the *Old England* out to the Far East for tea.[343] Despatching a ship involved finding and financing an outward-bound cargo - very often Manchester piece goods. It could be a stressful process, even for an experienced merchant. Thomas liked to keep a close eye on the proceedings in order to get his ships away as quickly as possible. As well as being a compulsive worker, he still found social occasions irresistible.

Queen Victoria visited Liverpool in 1851, in recognition of Liverpool's ascendency as a centre for trade. Elaborate preparations for the Royal visit had been made. The Queen arrived by boat, and the members of the Dock's Committee were given the privilege of welcoming her on the landing stage as she disembarked. Afterwards, the Queen made her way to the Town Hall where "the company assembled consisted of the mayor, the aldermen, and town councillors, the Docks Committee and many of the first merchants of the town, and a charming company of beautiful and elegant ladies".[344] It was precisely the type of occasion Thomas would not have wanted to miss, but his health was failing. People were incredibly eager to see their sovereign; there was a scramble for tickets for special events. So eager, that there was a 'most remarkable degree of selfishness' in trying to appropriate many of the coveted tickets.[345] In his younger days, Thomas might have contrived to get tickets by any means. It seems that this time, he did not. His name does not appear in the newspapers on the list of honoured guests. He was probably too ill to attend.

The festivities surrounding the royal visit ended with a grand ball at the town hall, attended by the mayor and other members of the corporation. 'Dancing commenced at about half past nine, and the rooms were soon crowded by a great number of our merchants and tradesmen, and their wives and daughters … there were plenty of sylph-like creatures tripping it on the light fantastic … The dancing was kept up to an early hour and the ball

219

formed one of the most delightful treats of this auspicious day'.[346]

* * *

In April 1852, in the Ripley's house in Abercromby Square, a young housemaid named Alice Shaw gave birth to a child. Frightened and unmarried, the girl crept into one of the bedrooms to give birth to her baby alone and unaided. The other servants didn't even realise she was pregnant. The first sign of trouble was that Alice didn't come down to eat at lunchtime. Someone was sent to look for her and she was found 'stretched on the floor of an upper room'. She was unconscious. Mrs Ripley was called and she immediately sent for the doctor. James Nottage arrived and he discovered traces of blood that led him to an adjoining room where he found a full-term baby girl in the wash hand basin, 'its face was pressed down in the water contained in the vessel, around its neck was tightly tied a flannel handkerchief.'[347]It must have been very distressing for Julia, who was childless, to discover that such a shocking event had occurred in her own home.

The doctor confirmed that the housemaid had just given birth, and that the baby was dead. Suspicion fell on the young girl; it was thought that the maid had suffocated her baby. An inquest was performed on the body of the child the same day, and it was decided that 'wilful murder' had taken place. Alice was arrested and committed for trial, but because of her 'weakly condition' she was placed under 'private surveillance'.

Later, when the case came to court, the terrified young housemaid was put in the dock, and even the judge was moved by her plight. He called for a chair for her.

It was a difficult and tragic case. The doctor was asked to testify. In a bid to help Alice Shaw, he claimed that the child might

220

not have been born alive. A conviction carried the death penalty. The jury retired to consider their verdict.

Infanticide was a social problem in Victorian England. This crime was extensively practised, especially in cities. Writing in the 1850s, William Scott said that 'in too many instances that young people 'keep company' on the understanding that marriage is to be postponed til it becomes necessary … if the man repents of his bargain, it seems the rule that infanticide should clear off the score.'[348] The case of the Ripley's housemaid was typical of many other cases at this time; 'when a girl of the labouring classes found herself pregnant, she did not fly to the law or make a fuss, she did her best to conceal her condition.'[349] Because the crime was punishable by death, juries were reluctant to find mothers guilty. Even Queen Victoria was said to be in favour of the removal of the death penalty for this crime. According to Duncan Crow, the 'medical evidence always tended to support the juries' bias.' This case was no exception. The young woman was acquitted.

* * *

In the spring of 1852 Thomas saw the arrival of his last shipments of tea. The *Panic* came home in February. She was damaged on the voyage home and had called in at Queenstown for repairs.[350] The *Mencius* brought him a quantity of tea in March.[351] The tea trade this spring was highly successful for him, and profits from it added considerably to his fortune. He wrote in a letter dated 5 August 1852, "My property *[has]* very much increased since November 1851."[352]

By August Thomas was at home in Abercromby Square, and he was a dying man. He had been thinking about what to do with the fortune he had amassed during his lifetime. He wanted to found a school similar to the Bluecoat School in Liverpool, for fatherless orphans. Julia fully supported his wishes. Thomas wanted his school to be built in Lancaster, where he was born. During Thomas's childhood, a Bluecoat School had existed in Lancaster, "for educating and clothing fifty boys".[353] No record of Thomas's own schooling has been found, but because his father died when Thomas was only eight, it is possible that he was educated there himself. The school operated between 1770 and 1816. Its closure would have been felt as a sad loss for the town. Thomas intended that his school should fill this gap. It would also serve as a long-standing memorial to his life's achievements, because he had no children of his own.

Unfortunately, the law as it stood prevented him from leaving all his money to charity.[354] When Thomas found this out he realised that the will he had made would not stand up in court. He evidently expected that his surviving relatives would contest his will. He went to his solicitor to make enquiries "as to the means of carrying out his charitable intention".[355] Firstly he was told that one solution would be to buy the land for the school himself, but this would have to be done at least twelve months before his death, and Thomas did not know if he had twelve months left to live. More importantly, and typically of Thomas, who always put business first, he objected that this plan "would abstract more than he could spare from his business".[356] After further discussions with Julia and his solicitor he had a second will drawn up to try to circumvent the problem. He had planned that most of his fortune should go directly to found the school. By the terms of the second will, however, his plan changed, he would have to leave almost *all* his money to Julia and rely upon her to found the school for him. He had great confidence in his wife's business sense. He trusted that Julia would remain loyal to him, and carry out his wishes.

With the second will, Thomas enclosed a letter to Julia in which he wrote "My dear wife, I have just signed my will … you will find that, after providing for my other relatives, liberally in my opinion, you are the residuary legatee … I did intend to have left you an annuity of 1,200 (pounds) per annum, with house and furniture in the Square, including horses, carriages, plate, pictures, linen, etc, which I believed you would consider sufficient for all purposes."[357] What the letter was intended to convey, was that he hoped that Julia would confine herself to the amount specified in the annuity, and use the rest to found his school. This intention becomes clearer still in the codicil to his will, dated 5 August 1852, where he writes "My property having very much increased since November 1851 I think it right to increase the annuity to 1,500 (pounds), which I hope … you will long enjoy." He ended his letter in this way: - "May God bless you my dear wife ever will be the prayer of your affectionate husband".[358]

Despite Thomas's determination that his school would be built, when his sisters got wind of the plan they were equally determined to thwart it. They wanted to see that money invested in their own family businesses. John Ripley also wanted a greater share of his brother's money because he had been living beyond his means in his mansion at Wallasey. Very little remained of the fortune John had made in the West Indies.[359]

In the last days of Thomas's life, his sister Ann insisted on seeing him on an almost daily basis. She harassed the dying man about the contents of his will. On the 13th August she questioned and cajoled him about the will hoping to convince him to change his mind. Thomas remained obdurate. He had set his heart on founding a school. He told Ann "I have left all to Julia", and turning to his wife, who was sitting at his bedside, he said, "I am sure, my dear, you will religiously, scrupulously, and conscientiously carry out my views". Julia 'acquiesced and took up his hand and kissed it'.[360] This romantic gesture showed that love remained alive between Thomas and Julia until they were parted. Seven days later Thomas Ripley was dead.

Commemorative bust of Thomas Ripley.

A notice appeared in the Liverpool Chronicle, announcing the death of 'Thomas Ripley Esquire, one of our most successful merchant princes in the East India and China trade.'[361] He died on the 20 August 1852 aged 61. Another eulogy claimed that he had 'secured for himself a high position among the merchants of Liverpool by his energy and integrity ... he was one of the first English merchants who embarked in the China trade. He soon ranked among the merchant princes of Liverpool, and his blameless character and benevolent disposition secured for him many friends'.[362]

Thomas Ripley's character and disposition were far more complex than his obituary suggests. He was something of a paradox. At different moments in his life he appeared as the ruthless shipowner - an ambitious businessman who could be

224

lavish one moment and miserly the next. In his personal life he was a romantic and loving husband, always generous to Julia. He could switch in an instant from taciturn committee member to jovial host. This cruel employer, who clapped his men in irons to crush their insubordination, could also be sentimental; he taught his pet canary to peck crumbs from his lips.

Whatever the truth about Thomas Ripley's character, he was certainly a popular man, well-liked and respected in Liverpool. Such a large number of his friends wanted to pay their last respects at his funeral that a special train was laid on to take the crowd of mourners from Liverpool railway station to Lancaster, where Thomas was to be buried.[363]

When the train steamed into Lancaster, local dignitaries joined the cortege, "the corpse being followed to its last resting place by the Mayor and Corporation of Lancaster, and a large number of friends".[364] The funeral was an impressive civic occasion in recognition of what Thomas had achieved and because of "the expectation at Lancaster that he intended to confer some benefit on that town". Thomas had made no secret of the fact that he was hoping to endow a charity school in the town where he was born. As a mark of respect, many of the local shopkeepers closed their premises while the funeral was taking place.[365]

Edward Doering, Thomas Ripley's old friend and neighbour, and Doering's business partner George Scholfield, were both at the funeral, and so was William Killick, another friend and business associate.[366] They were amongst the chief mourners, and would have travelled in one of the first carriages to follow the hearse. It was not the custom for women to attend funerals, so it is unlikely that Julia was among the mourners, nor would Thomas Ripley's sisters have attended. All the mourners would have been men. His sister Jane was represented by her husband, John Lomax.

Thomas was laid to rest in the cemetery of the parish church of Saint Mary's, Lancaster.

Whilst local people were praising Thomas for his generosity and awaiting the opening of the new school, some of his own relatives were still plotting to overturn these plans. Thomas's brother-in-law, John Lomax, spearheaded the opposition. In May 1853, Lomax filed a formal petition to contest the will.

* * *

Thomas left a fortune of £160,000 which amounts to approximately seven and a half million pounds in today's terms. In his own words, Thomas believed he had provided for his own relatives 'liberally'. In order to assess just how liberally he had provided for his surviving family, we must take a look at the terms of the will.[367]

Mary, the widow of Tom's brother Henry, received ten thousand pounds, which was then a huge sum. This may have been in recognition of the fact that Tom and Henry had been in partnership together for many years during the time that Thomas had begun to amass his fortune. Henry had been drowned at sea in 1841. Mary may have been one beneficiary who was satisfied with her bequest. She appears to have taken no part in the legal battle to overturn the will.

Tom's sister Ann Bland was also a widow. She received a house: number 10 Myrtle Street, and two hundred pounds for two years. Her children, Emma, Julia, Fanny, John and Joseph received eight thousand pounds between them, which was to be invested in railway shares and held in trust for them. At that time, Ann was already living in the Myrtle Street house with two of her daughters, Emma aged 33, and Frances aged 23, and their two servants, a cook and a housemaid.[368] Ann, as we know, was very dissatisfied with these bequests. She may have wished to live in more style and opulence, and she may have wanted more money to help establish her two sons in business.

Tom's other sister Jane Lomax, had daughters. Mary, Ellen and Clara were each left two thousand pounds. Nothing was left specifically to Jane, who was being supported by her husband, shipbuilder John Lomax, who filed the petition contesting the will.

John Ripley, Tom's brother, had squandered most of his own fortune, but still clung to his expensive lifestyle and mansion in Wallasey. His bequest was an annuity of two hundred and fifty pounds per annum. This sounds small compared with the other bequests, but would have enabled him to live out the rest of his retirement in comfort, if he had not been trying to maintain such a large establishment. He was dissatisfied with the annuity, and he united with the Lomax family to fight for more.

Julia's three sisters, Maria Reay, Harriet Pughe, and Charlotte Reay, each received a thousand pounds. It seems odd that at this point in the will, no mention was made of Julia's sister-in-law, the widow of her brother Charlie. Charles Lucas Reay, who had been working as a missionary in New Zealand, had died out there at the age of thirty-six in 1847. His wife Marianne and their young son Robert returned to England when Charlie died, and they were living in Walpole Street in Chelsea. It is known that Marianne was living on a grant from the Christian Missionary Society, and by 1851 she was in financial difficulties.[369] Julia's nephew Robert was by then a fatherless boy just like the children Thomas aspired to help in Lancaster. It seems inexplicable that he wasn't remembered in will.

Tom's oldest brother James was dead by this time, but a bequest was left to James' grandson, Herman Cords, who was living in the port of Hamburg. Herman received five hundred pounds.

All the servants were remembered; one hundred and fifty pounds was to be shared amongst them. Alfred Lacy, the Ripley's coachman, was singled out to receive a bequest of two hundred and fifty pounds, an astonishingly large amount to leave to a servant. This shows how much Tom valued this man's work and friendship. Lacy continue to serve loyally as Julia's coachman, for the rest of her life.[370]

Julia was appointed as one of the executors of her husband's will, indicating the great faith he had in her financial abilities. The other two executors were Henry Killick and George Sholfield, business associates and personal friends. They were liberally recompensed for their trouble with a bequest of five hundred pounds each.[371]

The bequests in the will were not even-handed in many cases. Why did Thomas insist that the money left to the Bland nephews and nieces should be invested on their behalf (even though none of them were children), when the money he left to Julia's sisters was given to them to use as they chose? Why did he leave the Lomax nieces two thousand pounds *each*, when the five Blands only got eight thousand between them? He left nothing to his sister Jane Lomax, who was married, and yet he left one thousand pounds to Julia's married sister, Harriet Pughe. Thomas bequeathed his money in the way that he did for reasons of his own, but inevitably this caused some discontentment amongst the beneficiaries.

Julia was left the residue of her husband's estate, which amounted to one hundred thousand pounds. Had she chosen to remarry, all of this would have become the legal property of her new husband. This was how the law stood until the Married

Women's Property Act was passed in 1882, which began the process of permitting married women to inherit in their own right, and was expanded by further legislation in 1893.[372] This was the risk that Thomas chose to take when leaving the money to her, in the hope that she would build his school. He told his solicitor that he "resolved to give the residue to Mrs Ripley, taking the chance of her applying it" as he might have wished.[373] It was a risk that few husbands took when making their wills prior to the Property Acts, because they knew that their wives would lose all rights over the money if they remarried. Julia was left in a very precarious situation.

*   *   *

The civil case, Lomax versus Ripley, finally came to court in December 1854. It was the week before Christmas when the case was heard in the vice chancellor's court. The *Lancaster Guardian* reported that the key question was "whether the gift of the residue to Mrs Ripley was void as being a gift with a secret understanding to found a charity, contrary to the Statute of Mortmain, or whether the gift to her was absolute and at her entire disposal."[374] In other words, because it was well known that Julia wanted to carry out her husband's last wishes, did this invalidate the will, even though Thomas had not made this a condition of the will?

Inhabitants of Lancaster were very anxious about the outcome and followed the case closely. They wanted the town to benefit from Thomas Ripley's fortune, as he had intended. A new school was a valuable asset in a town. The construction of the school buildings would provide years of employment for many men, since nineteenth century construction work was extremely labour intensive. Lancaster needed more work, since its shipping trade had gone into decline. The hope was that since Thomas had phrased his will very carefully, with no mention of the school, the will would be upheld.

The plaintiff, John Lomax, fighting to overturn the will, tried to prove that there was a secret pact between Thomas and Julia, which would invalidate the will.

Mrs Ann Bland was called as a witness. She gave evidence about the deathbed conversations concerning the school. She said that she and her brother Tom had often talked about his plans for the charity *in Julia's presence*.

The solicitor representing Lomax argued that "had not the said Julia Ripley ... made such promise as aforesaid, the said testator would not have left her his residuary legatee." Lomax's solicitor further claimed that "the residuary clause in the will was, in fact, inserted and made upon a secret understanding between the said testator and his wife."[375]

Julia Ripley in later life.

Mrs Ripley understood that her case would be lost if she admitted this. When she was called to give evidence, she "denied that she had made any promise to the testator to induce him to make her his residuary legatee". This was a cunning reply. She had evidently made a promise, but this promise was not made in order to *induce* Tom to make her his residuary legatee.

Next to be called was Tom's brother John. According to the paper, "Mr John Ripley, who supported the plaintiff's case" also claimed that his brother had talked about the school often, in the presence of Mrs Ripley. This appeared to support the argument that there was a secret pact.

Mrs Ripley had to deny any memory of these conversations. Unfortunately evidence emerged in the form of a letter from Julia to John Ripley, which almost destroyed her case. The letter, dated 6 April 1853, was read out in court. Julia had written

"I cannot help saying that one accusation is, that it is not my intention to carry into effect my husband's wishes as to the charity he intended to found at Lancaster … I declare to you it is my fixed determination, if it pleases God to spare my life, to carry out what you know as well as I do, were the wishes and intentions of my dear husband, had he lived to carry them out himself. On this subject I cannot say more."[376]

She had perhaps said too much! Julia was in a cleft stick. She had to deny making a secret pact with Tom, and yet she had wanted it to be known that she intended to go ahead with the school. She was not in a position to deny this. She had already "completed the purchase of certain land, and conveyed it to trustees upon trust for the charity".

The court case lasted six days in the Vice-Chancellor's Court. On the last day after hearing a long review of all the evidence the Vice-Chancellor reserved his judgement. When the court was reconvened the verdict was announced: the court ruled in Julia's favour. The people of Lancaster rejoiced and the bells of St Mary's Church were rung.[377] The last risk that Thomas Ripley ever took had paid off, just like so many of the other risks he took in his lifetime.

*   *   *

Julia went ahead with the task of carrying out Tom's wishes. In order to be near to the site of the school, Julia often stayed in Lancaster at the local vicarage. For the building of the school a large estate had been chosen, which consisted of a substantial house called Springfield Hall, and extensive grounds around it. Julia moved in to Springfield Hall on 17 February 1855, to oversee the construction of the school in the grounds of the estate.[378]

The following year Julia Ripley laid the foundation stone with great ceremony. There was a general holiday in Lancaster on that day, Monday 14 July 1856, the anniversary of her wedding day.[379] Afterwards there was a banquet for one hundred and fifty guests and also a dinner for two hundred workmen.[380] The banquet was held at the King's Arms Hotel. It was a very deliberate choice. The King's Arms had been the place where the Ripley brothers' bankruptcy sale had been held back in December 1817. The scene of the Ripleys' defeat was now the place where Julia celebrated their triumph.

26

How the Ripley Diary Survived

Julia lived in Lancaster for seventeen years. During this time she became well known in the town as a benefactor and supervised the running of the school. She lived in Springfield Hall, the large house in the school grounds, and spent the last years of her life surrounded by children. She made many new friends to whom she reminisced about her trip to the Far East, and she often lent her journal to people to read. So much so that in Lancaster an oral tradition persisted throughout the twentieth century that this journal had existed.

Julia lived until 1881, and by the terms of her will she left all her vast fortune to the school.[381] By astute investment, chiefly in the railways, Julia had amassed a fortune even larger than her husband's. Julia left her diary of the voyage to John Tyrer Preston, the headmaster of the school, knowing he would value it and preserve it. He and his wife Dorothy were close personal friends of Julia's. A year after Julia died John Preston resigned as headmaster. At the same time his wife also gave up her work as the school matron. The diary then disappeared without trace for more than eighty years.

Bust of Julia Ripley.

At a New Year's Eve party in 1975, four generations of the Hutchinson family had gathered together to celebrate. This was an ideal opportunity to draw up a family tree. Joy Hutchinson questioned the oldest member of the family, William Hutchinson, who was then nearly ninety. William offered to unlock an old metal box in which he kept documents and certificates. As Joy and William went through the contents of the box, Joy's eyes lighted on Julia's slim leather-bound diary. William explained that Julia Ripley was not his ancestor. So how had he come to be in possession of her diary?

He said that it came from the house of his great aunt, Dorothy Preston, after her death in 1914. William was helping to clear her house, and he and his wife Chrissie were invited to choose some items for themselves. While Chrissie was in the kitchen selecting some weighing scales and other household equipment, William was browsing through the books. Amongst these he found

Julia's journal. He'd heard about Julia Ripley and he knew about the school, which was still going strong at that time.

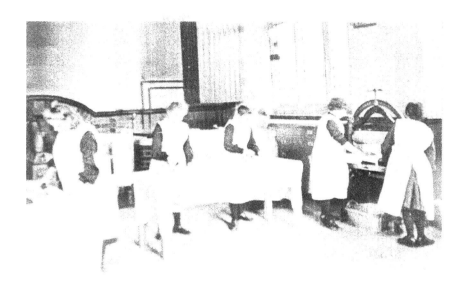

Edwardian girls learning how to do laundry at Ripley school.

Boys' band from Ripley school.

William Hutchinson recognised that Julia's journal was something that ought to be preserved. After reading the diary, William locked it up in the metal box to keep it safe. There it remained throughout his long working life as a Lancashire farmer. When he finally went into retirement in the South of England, the diary was one of the possessions that went with him.

Joy Hutchinson glanced through the pages and was shocked and amazed to see that the notorious Lintin was among the ports of call on the voyage. Joy was intrigued and fascinated by this voice from the 1830s. Oblivious to the New Year's Eve Party, she spent the rest of the evening totally absorbed in reading the diary. She longed to find out more about it and the woman who wrote it. So William gave the diary to Joy and suggested tracking down 'a very old mariner', not realising that over a hundred and forty years had elapsed since the diary was written which would make it impossible to find anyone alive who remembered those times. Instead Joy approached the National Maritime Museum at Greenwich for advice. Following up the leads they suggested, she embarked on her own journey of discovery that lasted for three years, and the story of the Ripley family began to emerge. Joy gathered together snippets of vital information from many different sources, and many different people.

Work on the research had to stop when Joy emigrated to New Zealand, and the journal went into obscurity again for another thirty years, but all this time it was one of her treasured possessions. She always hoped that one day the research would be completed and the diary published. The opportunity finally came in 2006. Marian Hutchinson was looking to find a project to work on after she had finished her doctorate. She regarded the journal as the find of a lifetime. She felt that such a unique document would be valued and enjoyed by a great many people.

Acknowledgements

I wish to acknowledge the help of the following people:

Liz Nicholls, Head Teacher of Ripley St. Thomas School, Lancaster
George Phythian, former Head Teacher of Ripley St. Thomas
William Hutchinson
F. B. Lothrop, Trustee of the Peabody Museum, Salem, Massachusetts
Gillian Gregg, Lancaster Museum
The staff of the Lancashire County Records Office, Preston
Neil Ripley Ker, University of Cambridge
Sheila Marriner, University of Liverpool
Ifor B. Powell, University of Cardiff
The staff of Merseyside County Museums, Liverpool
The staff of the Scottish Record Office, Edinburgh
Martin Barrow and Alan Reid, of Matheson and Co., for permission to consult the Jardine Matheson Archive.
John Wells, Department of Manuscripts and University Archives, and the staff at Cambridge University Library
Margeret Pamplin, of the University of Cambridge
Daphne Pipe and the staff at the National Maritime Museum, Greenwich, London
Lucy and William Fitchett, Australia
Andrew Rocco, Auckland, formatting, uploading and cover design
D.M Crook, former librarian of the Liverpool Medical Institution
The staff of Stevenage Museum
Bob Glover and Mrs. Carter, former students at Ripley Hospital
Wendy Ann Davey, who drew the sketches

238

The National Archives of Canada, Ottawa
The staff at the India Office Records, British Library, London
The staff at the Library of African and Oriental Studies
Michael Nash, Australasian Institute for Maritime Archaeology
Australia

Endnotes

[1] Thomas Ripley was baptised on the 28 November 1790. Bishop's transcripts of Register of Births, St Mary's Lancaster, held at CRO Preston.

[2] *Lancaster Gazette*, April 1808.

[3] Nancy Irwin and James Ripley married on 26 August 1787. Bishop's transcripts of Register of Marriages, St Mary's, Lancaster, held at CRO Preston.

[4] Bishop's transcripts of baptisms at St Mary's, Lancaster, 1787-1796, held at CRO Preston.

[5] Will of James Ripley, 1798, held at CRO Preston.

[6] Baptism of James Ripley, 10 March, 1754, St. Mary's Lancaster, Bishop's transcripts, CRO Preston.

[7] Register of Marriages, Lancaster Parish Church, 1801. Bishop's transcripts, Lancashire County Records Office, Preston.

[8] Property Valuation Register, 1808, CRO Preston.

[9] Will of James Ripley, 29 March 1798, Lancashire County Records Office, Preston.

[10] Details of the apprenticeship were supplied by Gillian Gregg, Lancaster Museum.

[11] The mill was situated at White Cross, Lancaster.

[12] *Lancaster Gazette*, 1806.

[13] *Essequebo and Demarary Gazette*, 29 December 1804.

[14] *Lancaster Gazette*, 7 January 1806.

[15] *Lancaster Gazette*, March 1806.

[16] Lancaster Gazette, 5 July 1808.

[17] Reports of the sale of two brigs in the merchants' coffee room. *Lancaster Gazette*, 1808.

[18] Lancaster Gazette, January 1806.

[19] Will of Edmund Pugh, proved 8 October 1805. Lancashire County Records Office, Preston.

[20] The Lancaster Poor Rate Books, 1811-12, County Records Office Preston.

[21] Holden's Directory, 1814-15.

[22] *Lancaster Gazette*, April, 1808.

[23] John Hughes, *Liverpool Banks and Bankers 1760 – 1837*, 1905.

[24] *Lancaster Guardian*, Saturday 13 December 1817.

[25] The Highway Book for Lancaster 1817, CRO Preston, shows that Mrs Pugh, the owner, had installed tenants.

[26] Lancaster Gazette, June 1808.

[27] Information provided by Lancaster Museum.

[28] T. Kaye, *The Stranger in Liverpool*, Liverpool, 1823, 7th edition.

[29] Gibson, John F., *Brocklebanks 1770-1950*, Liverpool, 1953. vol. 1.

[30] T. Kaye, *The Stranger in Liverpool*, Liverpool, 1823, 7th edition.

[31] 1819 Trade Directory of Liverpool.

[32] Kaye, *The Stranger in Liverpool*.

[33] *Liverpool Commercial Chronicle*, March 1826.

[34] Gibson, John F., *Brocklebanks 1770-1950*, Liverpool, 1953. vol. 1.

[35] Gibson, *Brocklebanks 1770-1950,* vol. 1.

[36] Gibson, *Brocklebanks 1770-1950*, vol. 1.

[37] Gibson, *Brocklebanks 1770-1950,* vol. 1.

[38] Hughes*, Liverpool Banks and Bankers*, 1905.

[39] The Ripley Diary, 22 July 1830.

[40] Correspondence of Ifor B. Powell, 10 July 1976.

[41] The Liverpool directories 1800-1829.

[42] William Reay, surgeon, married Charlotte Robinson in February 1799. Bishop's transcripts of the marriage register at Holy Trinity Church, Liverpool, held at County Records Office, Preston.

[43] T. H. Bickerton, *Medical History of Liverpool*, 1936.

[44] Maria was born in 1802. UK Census, 1861.

[45] Lottie Reay was born on 1 March 1817, and baptised in Liverpool.

[46] Correspondence of D. M. Crook, Librarian of the Liverpool Medical Institution, 17 May 1977.

[47] Letter attached to the will of William Lucas Reay, 1832, CRO Preston.

[48] *Gore's General Advertiser*, April 1823.

[49] T. Kaye, *The Stranger in Liverpool*, 1823.

[50] Announcement of marriage, *Liverpool Mercury*, 18 July 1823. Julia's age is given in the 1861 census.

[51] Austin, Harwood and Pyne, *Lancashire Illustrated*, London 1831.

[52] *Liverpool Directory*, 1827.

[53] *Gore's General Advertiser*, 5 June 1823.

[54] Lloyd's Lists.

[55] James Freme and Joseph M'Viccar were witnesses at the marriage of Julia's parents, Marriage Register, 4 February 1799, County Records Office, Preston.

[56] *Gore's General Advertiser*, 1823.

[57] *Gore's General Advertiser*, 23 January 1823.

[58] *Gore's Liverpool Advertiser*, January 1826.

[59] Lloyd's Lists 1834.

[60] Liverpool Commercial Chronicle, 13 May 1826.

[61] *Liverpool Times*, 16 July 1830.

[62] Shipping Register, vol. 187, Public Archives, Ottawa, Canada.

[63] Liverpool Commercial Chronicle, 22 December 1827.

[64] *Gore's Liverpool Advertiser*, October 1827.

[65] UK Census 1881.

[66] The Rumford Street address is listed in the Liverpool directory of 1829.

[67] T and J Brocklebank had their office in Rumford Street from 1825, Gibson, John F., *Brocklebanks 1770-1950*, Liverpool, 1953. vol. 1.

[68] Anthony Wild, The East India Company Book of Tea, Harper Collins, London, 1994.

[69] Jack Beeching, *The Chinese Opium Wars*, Hutchinson & Co., 1975, p. 19.

[70] Beeching, *The Chinese Opium Wars* p. 34.

[71] *Liverpool Times*, 13 January 1829.

[72] A report to this effect was issued as early as 1822. Correspondence of Sheila Marriner, University of Liverpool, 20 May 1976.

[73] *Liverpool Times*, 28 January 1829.

[74] *Liverpool Times*, 20 January 1829.

75 Gibson, John F., *Brocklebanks 1770-1950*, Liverpool, 1953. vol. 1.

76 Brian Inglis, *The Opium War*, Hodder and Stoughton, London, 1976, p. 34-35.

77 The Ripley Diary - Mr. Watson, 26 July 1830, Mr. Roe, 18 August 1830, 'The Doctor' 21 June 1830.

78 Brian Inglis, p. 76.

79 The Ripley Diary and correspondence of S. M. Riley, Merseyside County Museums, Liverpool, 11 March 1976.

80 *Liverpool Albion*, 31 May 1830

81 *Singapore Chronicle,* 6 December 1830.

82 An advertisement for Maynard's Outfitting, *India Register*, 1830, at the India Office Library.

83 *India Register*, 1830.

84 Diaries of Captain and Mrs Sherwood, *Life and Times of Mrs Sherwood*, London: Wells Gardner, Darton & Co., Ltd., [1910].

85 An advertisement for Maynard's Outfitting, *India Register*, 1830, at the India Office Library.

86 The Ripley diary, 4 July 1830.

87 Gore's General Advertiser, May 1823.

88 Sir Pertinax MacSycophant was a famous burlesque character created by Charles Macklin for his play *Men of the World* (1781).

89 Julia is quoting from Sir Thomas Moore's poem *Common Sense and Genius.*

90 The Shipping Register, vol. 187, Public Archives Canada.

91 James Horsburgh, *Directions for Sailing to and from the East Indies, China, etc.,* London, 1817.

92 L. A. Mills, *British Malaya, 1824-67,* Singapore: Methodist Publishing House, 1925.

93 UK Census, 1851.

94 Mr. Forrester was of A.L. Forrester and Co., Mr. Watson was of Maclaine, Watson and Co., Batavia. Correspondence of Ifor B. Powell, 10 July 1976.

95 The gardens of Buitenzorg/Bogor near Jakarta remain a tourist attraction to the present day. They had been laid out in 1817 by C. G. E. Runwardt, an Amsterdam professor of botany. The house was destroyed by earthquake in 1832.

96 These stones may have been the ruins at Batu Tulis, which

means 'inscribed rock', where the remains of the ancient capital of the kingdom of Pajajaran can be seen. The monument is a slab of stone bearing an inscription, which has now been translated from ancient Palawa script. It proclaims the eminence of Prabu Guru Dewata Prana.

[97] Correspondence of Ifor B. Powell, 10 July 1976.

[98] Correspondence of Ifor B. Powell, 10 July 1976.

[99] The population of Singapore was 20,000 according to the 1833 Census, of which only 119 were Europeans.

[100] Robert Ibbetson was Resident of Singapore from 1830-1833. He was appointed by the British EIC to administer the colony of Singapore.

[101] At this time all the officers were British, and there were also 150 Indian Sepoy. Correspondence of E. Talbot Rice, National Army Museum, London, 5 July 1976.

[102] George Stott was the son of a fustian manufacturer from Manchester. Correspondence of E. Talbot Rice, National Army Museum, London, 5 July 1976.

[103] In 1828 Montagu assumed command of the *Crocodile*, which was to remain in the East Indies until the summer of 1832. Correspondence of the Curator of the Stevenage Museum, Hertfordshire. 15 July 1976.

[104] For more information on this see C. N. Parkinson, *Trade in the Eastern Seas 1793-1813,* 1937.

[105] The Singapore Chronicle, 9 January 1831.

[106] Correspondence of Ifor B. Powell, 10 July 1976.

[107] Correspondence of Ifor B. Powell, 31 July 1976.

[108] Correspondence of Ifor B. Powell, 10 July 1976.

[109] Lloyd's Register of Ships.

[110] UK Census 1851.

[111] Lloyd's Lists.

[112] Navy Lists, 1830, National Maritime Museum, Greenwich.

[113] The Singapore Chronicle, January 1831.

[114] Thomas Stamford Raffles, *History of Java*, 1817.

[115] David Abeel, *Journal of a Residence in China and the Neighboring Countries from 1829 to 1833*, New York, Levitt, Lord and Co., 1834. Abeel was a minister of the Reformed Dutch Church.

[116] David Abeel, *Journal of a Residence in China.*

[117] David Abeel, *Journal of a Residence in China*.

[118] Correspondence of Alan Reid of Matheson & Co., 16 May 1976.

[119] Michael Greenberg, *British Trade and The Opening of China 1800-42,* Cambridge, University Press, 1969.

[120] Jack Beeching, *The Chinese Opium Wars*, Hutchinson and Co., 1975, p. 42.

[121] Mrs. Turner was the wife of Richard Turner of Turner & Co. Correspondence of F. B. Lothrop, 3 January 1977.

[122] Thomas Fox had recently arrived in Macao from England. Journal of Harriett Low, cited in correspondence of F. B. Lothrop (Trustee of the Peabody Museum, Salem Massachusetts, 11 May 1977.

[123] *Canton Register*, 4 July 1831.

[124] Brian Inglis, *The Opium War*, Hodder and Stoughton, London, 1976, p. 77.

[125] The Turners' house had a fine view of the Jesuit Church of St Paul's, which was then over two hundred years old, but in 1836 it was destroyed by a fire and only the façade remained as a tourist attraction. Correspondence of F. B. Lothrop, 3 January 1977.

[126] Henry and Sidney Berry-Hill, *George Chinnery*, F. Lewis, Leigh-on-Sea, 1963.

[127] Cited in correspondence of F. B. Lothrop, 3 January 1977.

[128] John Francis Davis was the second member of the EIC Select Committee and was later to become one of the first governors of Hong Kong in 1844. Jack Beeching, p. 168.

[129] Charles Majoribanks was President of the EIC Select Committee. EIC Register.

[130] John Bensley Thornhill was a writer employed by the EIC. EIC Register.

[131] James Frederick Nugent Daniell was the third member of the EIC Select Committee. EIC Register.

[132] Brian Inglis, *The Opium War*, p.17.

[133] Jack Beeching, *The Chinese Opium Wars*, p. 37.

[134] The Pearl River is now the Zhujiang and flows into the Boca Tigris Estuary.

[135] Correspondence of Alan Reid of Matheson & Co., 5 July 1976.

[136] Nathan Allen, *The Opium Trade*, Lowell Massachusetts, 1853.

[137] James Holman, 'Travels in China, 1830', in *A Voyage Round the World, Volume One, Including Travels in Africa, Asia, Australasia, America, etc., etc., from 1827 to 1832.*

[138] I. Hsu, *The Rise of Modern China*, Oxford University Press, 1970, p. 201.

[139] Mrs. Morrison was the wife of the famous missionary, Dr. Morrison, whose translation of the bible into Chinese was published in 1823 by the Anglo-Chinese College in Malacca.

[140] Fan, Fa-ti, *British Naturalists in Qing China, Science, Empire and Cultural Encounter,* Harvard University Press, Cambridge, Massachusetts, 2004, p. 21.

[141] Journal of Harriett Low, 3 September 1831, cited in correspondence of F. B. Lothrop, 2 January 1977.

[142] I. Hsu, *The Rise of Modern China*, Oxford University Press, 1970, p. 201.

[143] Journal of Harriett Low, 15 May 1830, cited in the correspondence of F. B. Lothrop, 3 June 1977.

[144] Journal of Harriett Low, 3 September 1831, cited in the correspondence of F. B. Lothrop, 27 July 1977. J. B. Thornhill was a writer employed by the EIC. EIC Register.

[145] Correspondence of F. B. Lothrop (Peabody Museum), 11 May 1977.

[146] Thomas Allport belonged to the English merchant house, Thomas Dent & Co.

[147] The *EIC Register*, 1831.

[148] Journal of Harriett Low, cited in correspondence of F. B. Lothrop, 3 January 1977.

[149] Brian Inglis, p. 106.

[150] J. F. N. Daniell was a supercargo and sub-treasurer of the EIC in China.

[151] Hugh Hamilton Lindsay was also a supracargo, and had been a writer for the EIC. *EIC Register* 1831.

[152] Correspondence of F. B. Lothrop, 11 May 1977.

[153] Journal of Harriett Low, cited in correspondence of F. B. Lothrop (Peabody Museum, Salem Massachusetts), 2 December 1977.

[154] Hardy's *Register of Ships*, 1831.

[155] Letterbooks of Jardine Matheson & Co., 12 August 1831.

[156] Journal of Harriett Low, 5 September 1832, cited in Correspondence of F. B. Lothrop (Peabody Museum, Salem Massachusetts) 8 August 1977.

[157] According to F. B. Lothrop, to take an ordinary fastboat from Macao to Lintin would require a Chinese visa, correspondence of F. B. Lothrop, 6 July 1977.

[158] Correspondence of Ifor B. Powell, 10 July 1976.

[159] Correspondence of Ifor B. Powell, 15 July 1976.

[160] Correspondence of Ifor B. Powell, 31 July 1976.

[161] According to Powell, the *Feejee* was consigned to Robert Wise & Co., headed in Manila by John Benjamin Butler.

[162] Correspondence of Ifor B. Powell, 15 July 1976.

[163] Thomas Cellar, Hermann von Meyer, *Frankfurt citizen and founder of the vertebrate animal palaeontology in Germany*, Stork, Gerhard, 2001.

[164] *Hampshire Advertiser*, 23 April 1832.

[165] Correspondence of E. Talbot Rice, Research and Information Officer, National Army Museum, London, 9 June 1976.

[166] The Archbishop was making his official entry after receiving the pallium, a white garment, the symbol of his office. Emma Helen Blair and James Alexander Robertson, *The Philippine Islands, 1493-1898*, Cleveland, A. H. Clark Company, 1903.

[167] Correspondence of Ifor B. Powell, 15 July 1976.

[168] Chinese Courier, December 1831.

[169] Records of William R. Bowers & Co., (Collection 24), G. W. Blunt Library, Mystic Seaport, Connecticut.

[170] Singapore Chronicle, 11 November 1831.

[171] Singapore Chronicle, 11 November 1831.

[172] *R. MacMiking, Recollections of Manila and the Philippines during 1848, 1849, and 1850*, Manila Filipiana Book Guild, 1967.

[173] Borradailes, Thompson, & Pillans & Co., of Rosebank, Rondebosch, was a house of trade carrying on business in Cape Town. The company traded in wine, tea, oxen, grain, and gunpowder. The partners were John Watson Borradailes, George Thompson and Charles Stuart Pillans (who left many descendents).

[174] C. M'Call Theal, *History of South Africa*, 1828-1846,

Sonnenschein.

175 Count E.A.D. de Las Cases was an early biographer of Napoleon, and accompanied him in his exile on St Helena. Las Cases wrote *Memorial de Ste Hélène*, 5 vols., London and Paris, 1823, often republished and translated.

176 Frank McLynn, *Napoleon, a Biography,* Random House, UK, 2002.

177 McLynn, *Napoleon*, p. 639.

178 Bishop's transcripts of the Register of Baptism of St Anne, Liverpool, March 1817, held at CRO Preston Lancashire.

179 J. G. Wood, *New Illustrated Natural History*, Reptiles and Fishes, George Routledge, London and New York, 1874.

180 Stephen Fox, *Transatlantic: Samuel Cunard, Isambard Brunel, and the Great Atlantic Steamships,* Harper Collins, 2004.

181 Bishop's transcripts of Registers of St. Mary Lancaster, held at County Records Office Preston.

182 Asiatic cholera had arrived in England in late 1831, adding to the dangers of life in London.

183 Shipping News, *Liverpool Times*, 24 April 1832.

184 Ships entered for loading, *Liverpool Times*, 23 October 1832 and 11 December 1832.

185 Liverpool Trade Directories, 1829 and 1834 cited in a letter from S. M Riley of the Merseyside County Museums, 9 January 1976.

186 Index to Lloyd's surveys, 1832.

187 Robert Ker to John Ker, 6 June 1832. Letterbook of Thomas Ripley Ker, cited in the correspondence of Neil Ripley Ker, 23 May 1976.

188 *Liverpool Times*, 8 January 1833.

189 *Liverpool Times* 12 February 1833.

190 *Liverpool Times* 24 April 1833.

191 *Liverpool Times* 21 May 1833.

192 *Liverpool Times* 11 February 1834.

193 *Liverpool Times*, 11 March, 1834.

194 Commissionary records of the Sheriff Court of Midlothian, SC70/1/49, pp. 56-9, cited in a letter from M D Young of the Scottish Record Office, Edinburgh, 16 June 1976.

195 Testament of Margaret Duthie, SC70/1/49.

[196] Hardy's Register of Ships, 1832.

[197] Information on Rev. Charles Lucas Reay, Kinder Library, Auckland, New Zealand.

[198] Will of William Ripley, 1834, Lancaster Records Office, Preston, Lancashire.

[199] *Liverpool Times*, 17 March 1835.

[200] B. Inglis, *The Opium War*, p. 76.

[201] B. Inglis, p. 93.

[202] B. Inglis, p. 106.

[203] Letter from James Matheson to John Macvicar, 4 August 1832, private letterbook of James Matheson, Jardine Matheson archive, Cambridge University Library.

[204] Letter from James Matheson to John Macvicar, 9 August 1832, ibid.

[205] *Liverpool Times*, vessels entered for loading, 12 May 1835.

[206] *Liverpool Times*, shipping news, 23 June 1835.

[207] Correspondence of Alan Reid of Matheson & Co., 5 July 1976.

[208] *Liverpool Times*, 26 May 1835.

[209] *Liverpool Mercury*, shipping news, 1 January 1836.

[210] Gore's *Liverpool Advertiser*, December 1836.

[211] *Liverpool Mercury*, 10 June 1836.

[212] *Liverpool Mercury*, October 1836.

[213] *Liverpool Mercury*, October 1836.

[214] Jack Beeching, *The Chinese Opium Wars*, p. 37.

[215] Brian Inglis, *The Opium War*, p. 62.

[216] History Departments of Futan and Shanghai Universities, *The Opium War*, Peking, 1976, p. 9.

[217] History Departments of Futan and Shanghai Universities, *The Opium War*, p. 16.

[218] *Gore's Liverpool Advertiser*, December 1837.

[219] *Gore's Liverpool Advertiser*, December 1837.

[220] *Gore's Liverpool Advertiser*, 19 June 1837.

[221] *Mercantile Journal* 1838, January.

[222] Lin's letter to Queen Victoria: Peter Fay, *The Opium War 1840-1842*, Chapel Hill, NC: University of North Carolina Press, 1975, p. 143, cited in W. Travis Hanes, *The Opium Wars*, Illinois, Sourcebooks, 2002, p. 39.

[223] Lin to Victoria, cited in Travis Hanes, p. 40.

224 Inglis, *The Opium War*, p. 118.

225 Travis Hanes, p. 42-3.

226 Inglis, *The Opium War*, p. 172.

227 Correspondence of F. B. Lothrop, 3 January 1977.

228 Elmer Loines (ed.), *China Trade Postbag of the Seth Low Family of Salem, New York, 1829-1873,* letter dated 17 April 1839 from Abeel Low to his sister Harriett Hillard.

229 Gore's General Advertiser, 7 November 1839. *Tigris* belonged to T & J Brocklebank.

230 Letter from Robert Ker to John Ker, Letterbook 1, Robert Ker papers, from correspondence from Neil Ripley Ker, 14 June 1976.

231 Gore's Liverpool Advertiser, May 1838.

232 Jack Beeching, The Opium Wars, p. 97.

233 Brian Inglis, The Opium War, p. 125.

234 Travis Hanes, p. 60.

235 Jack Beeching, The Chinese Opium Wars, p. 89.

236 Travis Hanes, p. 63.

237 Charles Gutzlaff, *China Opened*, 1838.

238 *Liverpool Mercury*, 28 April 1832.

239 Travis Hanes, p. 65.

240 The Hobart Town Courier and Van Diemen's Land Gazette, 20 March, 1840, p.4.

241 Parbury's Oriental Herald and Colonial Intelligencer, vol IV, July to December, 1839.

242 The Hobart Town Courier and Van Diemen's Land Gazette, 20 March, 1840, p.4.

243 William Ewart Gladstone, cited in Paul Knapland, Gladstone's Foreign Policy, 1970, p.6

244 Travis Hanes, p. 68.

245 Travis Hanes, p. 87.

246 Travis Hanes, p. 94.

247 Ker to MacMicking, Letterbook 1 of Robert Ker, cited in a letter from Neil Ripley Ker, dated 14 June 1976.

248 Ker to MacMicking, 26 January, 1840. Letterbook 1 of Robert Ker, cited in a letter from Neil Ripley Ker, dated 14 June 1976.

249 *Canton General Price Current*, 18 July 1840.

250 Ker to MacMicking, Letterbook 1 of Robert Ker, cited in a

letter from Neil Ripley Ker, dated 14 June 1976.

251 *Canton General Price Current*, 22 August 1840.

252 Ker to MacMicking, Letterbook 1 of Robert Ker, cited in a letter from Neil Ripley Ker, 14 June 1976.

253 R. Ker to E. Doering, 8 January, 1840, Letterbook 1 of Robert Ker, cited in correspondence from Neil Ripley Ker, 14 June 1976.

254 London Mercantile Journal, 24 December 1840.

255 Beeching, *The Chinese Opium Wars*.

256 *Canton General Price Current*, 22 May 1841.

257 Robert to MacMicking, 26 January 1840, Letterbook 1 of Robert Ker, cited in a letter from Neil Ripley Ker, 14 June 1976.

258 R. Ker to MacMicking, 26 January 1840.

259 R. Ker to Edward Doering, 9 December 1842. Letterbook 1

260 Biographical information on Charles Lucas Reay, Kinder Library, Auckland, New Zealand.

261 James Stack cited in Reay Reunion Publication, cited in correspondence of Melissa Vinson, 23 February 2007.

262 Frances Knight, *The Nineteenth Century Church and English Society*, Cambridge University Press, 1995, p. 134.

263 Inglis, *The Opium War*, p. 129.

264 Cited in a letter from S. M. Riley, Department of Maritime History, Merseyside County Museums, Liverpool, 9 January 1976

265 Liverpool Customs Bills of Entry, 1841, Merseyside County Museums.

266 Liverpool Customs Bills of Entry, 1841.

267 *Liverpool Times*, 20 July 1841.

268 *Liverpool Times*, 20 July 1841.

269 *Liverpool Mercury*, April 1836.

270 Minutes of the Docks Committee 1837, Liverpool.

271 *Liverpool Times*, 23 February 1841.

272 *Liverpool Times*, 16 March 1841.

273 Travis Hanes, *The Opium Wars*, p. 143.

274 Hanes, p.143.

275 Inglis, *The Opium War*, p. 205

276 Thomas Ripley to Messrs. Jardine and Matheson, 5 August 1843, Jardine Matheson Archive.

277 Ripley to Messrs. Jardine and Matheson, 5 August, 1843.

278 Correspondence of Ifor B. Powell, 31 July 1976.

279 UK Census 1851.

280 UK Census, 1851.

281 Correspondence of S. M. Riley, Department of Maritime History, Merseyside County Museums, 22 July 1976.

282 Census 1851.

283 London Mercantile Journal, February 1842.

284 Liverpool Customs Bills of Entry, March 1842.

285 Liverpool Customs Bills of Entry, June 1842.

286 Liverpool Customs Bills of Entry, October 1842.

287 Liverpool Customs Customs Bills of Entry, November, December, 1842.

288 *Gores Liverpool Advertiser*, January 1844.

289 Lloyd's Register, cited in correspondence from Daphne Pipe, National Maritime Museum, 16 June 1977.

290 *Gore's Liverpool Advertiser*, December 1844.

291 Correspondence from J. S. Rebecca, 18 October 1976.

292 Will of Thomas Ripley, 1852.

293 Sydney Herald, January 1845.

294 *Sydney Herald*, January 1845.

295 Liverpool Bills of Entry, June 1845.

296 Liverpool Customs Bills of Entry, January 1845.

297 Mercantile Journal, March 1845.

298 Liverpool Customs Bills of Entry, 1845.

299 Liverpool Customs Bills of Entry, April 1845.

300 Liverpool Bills of Entry, November 1845.

301 Liverpool Customs Bills of Entry, January, June, 1846.

302 Liverpool Bills of Entry, October, 1846.

303 'The Opening of Albert Dock', supplement to the *Liverpool Courier,* 5 August 1846, p.9.

304 'The Opening of Albert Dock', supplement to the *Liverpool Courier,* 5 August 1846, p.9.

305 Correspondence of S. M Riley, Merseyside County Museums, 7 December 1976.

306 Liverpool Mercury, 13 February 1847.

307 Correspondence of S. M Riley, Department of Maritime History, Merseyside County Museums, 7 December 1976.

308 Liverpool Customs Bills of Entry, February 1847.

309 *London Mercantile Journal*, 3 February 1848.

[310] *Liverpool Times* 30 November 1847.

[311] Richardson, Lesley, 'Paremata Te Wahapiro, Te Kiore fl. 1822-1845' *Dictionary of New Zealand Biography*, volume one, Wellington, 1990.

[312] Correspondence of Lucy Fitchett, 22 December 1977.

[313] Geoffrey Blainey, *The Tyranny of Distance*, Pan Macmillan Sydney, 2001, (first published 1966 by Sun Books) p. 162.

[314] Correspondence of Lucy Fitchett, 2 April 1978.

[315] Correspondence of William Fitchett, 7 February 1850.

[316] Geelong District Archives.

[317] Correspondence of William Fitchett, 7 February 1850.

[318] Geoffrey Blainey, *The Tyranny of Distance*, p. 163.

[319] Geoffrey Blainey, *The Tyranny of Distance*, p. 163.

[320] Correspondence of William Fitchett, 7 February 1850.

[321] Correspondence of Lucy Fitchett, 22 December 1977.

[322] Correspondence of William Fitchett, 7 February 1850.

[323] Fitchett, 7 February 1850.

[324] Fitchett, 7 February 1850.

[325] Lucy Fitchett, 2 April 1978.

[326] Fitchett, 7 February 1850.

[327] David R. MacGregor, *The Tea Clippers*, Conway Maritime Press, London, 1983, p. 50.

[328] Liverpool Customs Bills of Entry, September 1849.

[329] Liverpool Customs Bills of Entry, April 1849.

[330] Liverpool Customs Bills of Entry, January 1850.

[331] MacGregor, *The Tea Clippers*, p. 45

[332] Correspondence of Alan Reid, 5 June 1976.

[333] Correspondence of W. S. Brown to S. G. Rathbone , 1850 cited in *History of the Rathbones*.

[334] *The Tea Clippers*, p. 45.

[335] Liverpool Customs Bills of Entry, January 1850.

[336] *The Tea Clippers*, p. 226.

[337] Shipping Intelligence, *Daily Alta*, California, 5 August 1851.

[338] *Hobart Town Courier*, 30 June 1853.

[339] M. Nash, 1990. 'Survey of the Historic Ship Litherland (1834-1853)', *Bulletin of the Australian Institute for Maritime Archaeology* 14 (1): 13-20.

[340] *Liverpool Chronicle*, August 1852.

[341] Correspondence of S. M. Riley, Merseyside County

Museums, 22 July 1976.

342 Liverpool Customs Bills of Entry, February 1852.

343 Liverpool Customs Bills of Entry, August, 1852.

344 Thomas Baines *History of the Commerce and Town of Liverpool and of the rise of Manufacturing Industry in the Adjoining Counties*, London, Longman and Co., 1858.

345 *Liverpool Courier,* 8 October 1851.

346 *Liverpool Mercury Supplement*, 10 October 1851.

347 *Liverpool Chronicle*, 3 April 1852, p. 4.

348 Rev. W. Scott, cited in Duncan Crow, *The Victorian Woman*, 1971.

349 Cited in Duncan Crow, *The Victorian Woman*, 1971.

350 David R. MacGregor, *The Tea Clippers*, p. 226.

351 Liverpool Customs Bills of Entry, March 1852.

352 *Lancaster Guardian*, 23 December 1854, p.8.

353 Baines, *History of Lancaster*, 1858.

354 The terms of the medieval statute of Mortmain rendered Thomas Ripley's first will illegal. Correspondence of Gillian Gregg, Lancaster City Council Museum, 2 February 1976.

355 *Lancaster Guardian*, 23 December 1854, p. 8.

356 *Lancaster Guardian*, 23 December 1854, p. 8.

357 *Lancaster Guardian*, 23 December 1854.

358 *Lancaster Guardian*, 23 December 1854.

359 Correspondence of J. S. Rebecca, 25 June 1976.

360 *Lancaster Guardian* 23 December 1854.

361 *Liverpool Chronicle*, August 1852.

362 *Lancaster Guardian*, 5 November 1864, p. 3

363 Information obtained form Lancaster Museum.

364 *Lancaster Guardian*, 5 November 1864, p. 3

365 Lancaster Guardian, 23 December 1854, p. 8.

366 Correspondence of Ifor B. Powell, 31 July 1976.

367 Will of Thomas Ripley 1852.

368 1851 UK Census.

369 Library of Kinder House, Auckland, New Zealand.

370 Will of Julia Ripley, 1881. Lancashire County Records Office Preston.

371 Will of Thomas Ripley, proved at Chester, 2 September 1852.

372 The first Married Women's Property Act (1882) permitted

women to inherit from a parent, and the second Act (1893) granted them greater rights over property acquired in other ways, e.g. during a previous marriage or through their own earnings.

373 Lancaster Guardian, 23 December 1854, p. 8.

374 Lancaster Guardian, 23 December 1854, p. 8.

375 *Lancaster Guardian*, 23 December 1854, p. 8.

376 *Lancaster Guardian*, 23 December 1854, p. 8.

377 Correspondence of Gillian Gregg, 2 February 1976, Lancaster City Council Museum.

378 Information provided by Gillian Gregg of Lancaster City Council Museum.

379 *Lancaster Guardian*, July 1856.

380 *Lancaster Observer*, 26 October 1917. Correspondence of Gillian Gregg, 2 February 1976, Lancaster City Council Museum

381 Will of Julia Ripley, 1881.

12274946R00140

Made in the USA
Charleston, SC
24 April 2012